ON DOING
LOCAL HISTORY

About the Series
The American Association for State and Local History Book Series publishes technical and professional information for those who practice and support history, and addresses issues critical to the field of state and local history. To submit a proposal or manuscript to the series, please request proposal guidelines from AASLH headquarters: AASLH Book Series, 1717 Church St., Nashville, Tennessee 37203. Telephone: (615) 320-3203. Fax: (615) 327-9013. Web site: www.aaslh.org.

About the Organization
The American Association for State and Local History (AASLH) is a nonprofit educational organization dedicated to advancing knowledge, understanding, and appreciation of local history in the United States and Canada. In addition to sponsorship of this book series, the Association publishes the periodical *History News*, a newsletter, technical leaflets and reports, and other materials; confers prizes and awards in recognition of outstanding achievement in the field; and supports a broad education program and other activities designed to help members work more effectively. To join the organization, contact: Membership Director, AASLH, 1717 Church St., Nashville, Tennessee 37203.

ON DOING LOCAL HISTORY

SECOND EDITION

CAROL KAMMEN

A Division of Rowman & Littlefield Publishers, Inc.
Walnut Creek • Lanham • New York • Oxford

AltaMira Press
A Member of the Rowman & Littlefield Publishing Group
1630 North Main Street, #367
Walnut Creek, CA 94596
www.altamirapress.com

Rowman & Littlefield Publishers, Inc.
4720 Boston Way
Lanham, MD 20706

PO Box 317
Oxford
OX2 9RU, UK

Copyright © 2003 by AltaMira Press

British Library Cataloguing in Publication Information Available

Library of Congress Cataloging-in-Publication Data

Kammen, Carol, 1937–
    On doing local history / Carol Kammen.—2nd ed.
        p. cm.—(American Association for State and Local History book series)
Includes bibliographical references and index.
    ISBN 0-7591-0252-X (alk. paper)—ISBN 0-7591-0253-8 (pbk. : alk. paper)
1. United States—History, Local—Handbooks, manuals, etc. 2. Local history. I. Title. II. Series.
E180.K28 2003
973'.07'2—dc21

                                                    2002011821

Printed in the United States of America

∞™ The paper used in this publication meets the minimum requirements of American National Standard for Information Sciences—Permanence of Paper for Printed Library Materials, ANSI/NISO Z39.48-1992.

This book is for Michael

Contents

Foreword by Terry A. Barnhart, ix

Preface to the Second Edition, xiii

Introduction, 1

CHAPTER 1

Local History's Past, 11

Coda to Chapter 1: Revising What Is Held as True, 42

CHAPTER 2

Thinking about History, 47

Coda to Chapter 2: Censorship, 59

CHAPTER 3

The Subjects of Local History, 65

Coda to Chapter 3: Journalists and Historians, 86

CHAPTER 4

Researching Local History, 91

Coda to Chapter 4: When Being Right Is Not Good Enough, 115

CHAPTER 5

Giving Back, 121

Coda to Chapter 5: The Great Document Exchange, 138

CHAPTER 6

The Local Historian, 143

Coda to Chapter 6: Adult Local History Workshops, 156

CHAPTER 7

The Past That Was Yesterday, 161

Coda to Chapter 7: One Last Thing, 179

Index, 185

About the Author, 189

Foreword

The confessions of local historians too often take on the air of apologias or special pleadings for why their works are important. It is more useful, perhaps, to reclaim the prominent place that local history has held in American letters since the birth of the republic and to avoid the common fallacy of speaking about local and national histories in dichotomous terms. Local history holds great value for many different audiences, each of which brings its own expectations, assumptions, and interests to the task of "doing" local history.

No single set of concerns or approaches defines local history as a field of historical inquiry. It would be as presumptuous as it would be incomplete to fashion a single definition that would serve *all* practitioners of local history. Local history is a big tent—the democratic province of both amateurs and professionals—and local historians are as diverse as their audiences. No one has a better appreciation or understanding of those realities than Carol Kammen, and certainly there is no one with more authority to speak of them. Her first edition of *On Doing Local History* (1986) has been a faithful companion to those seeking to place local history within a broader theoretical and methodological context and to those demonstrating its larger claims to attention. This second edition will doubtless receive the same favored status, and the American Association for State and Local History Book Series and its publishing partner, AltaMira Press, have done a professional service by presenting it to the public.

Local history in the United States has its own past and a rich historiography. When Hermann Ernst Ludewig wrote a bibliographical essay titled *Literature of American Local History* in 1846, the number of writings on the subject was already voluminous. A comparison of that literature with the sustained interest in American local history in the twentieth and twenty-first centuries shows how successive generations of Americans have defined, approached, and practiced local history. Each of those changes in interpretive paradigms is a window into American cultural history—national and local—that helps clarify many of the ambiguities, paradoxes, and contradictions of the American experience. Historians who concern themselves with delineating the characteristics of local politics, patterns of culture, the construction of local and regional identities, and the inner workings of specific communities want to know whether localized experience meets our expectations of historical reality. Which of our assumptions about national traditions ring true and which are in need of revision? What was the angle of vision from the periphery of national life as well as from its political and cultural centers? What are the meaningful connections between regionalism and nationalism? Why are local history and national history often spoken of in antithetical terms?

Local historians in the United States have shown great interest in founding museums, archives, and historical societies; in preserving historic sites; and in constructing historical narratives across many generations. Museums and historical societies were the first purveyors of public history, and they continue to keep faith with their founding missions and time-honored interests. They have gathered and preserved invaluable collections of manuscripts, files of newspapers, and printed sources with local imprints that are the building blocks of the historian's craft. These localized sources are the foundations of historical journals published by state historical societies and historical editing projects that continue to make original contributions to knowledge. Local history is, indeed, a community of interest and a common enterprise as well as a body of literature.

But how often are local historians gently, engagingly, and effectively challenged to think about what they do and why and how they do it? The second and revised edition of Carol Kammen's *On Doing Local History*, like the first edition, does that by continuing to make us think. New materials have been added without sacrificing what is timeless and true in the materials carried forward from the first edition. The author's revisions reflect changes that have occurred in the field of history since the publication of the original edition and offer thoughtful perspectives on the themes, topics, approaches, and concerns of local historians past and present. *On Doing Local History* chronicles the history of local history in the United States, deconstructs the processes by which one generation revises what has been previously held true about the past, and provides concrete examples of how local history is actually done. This book is certainly practical, but it is much more than a how-to-do-local-history manual, any number of which have appeared over the years. It also probes deeply into the questions involved in presenting the past to public audiences and into what history at the grass roots ultimately means for communities and individuals.

Terry A. Barnhart
History Department
Eastern Illinois University

Preface to the Second Edition

Revising a book, I have just discovered, is a curious form of balancing. It is like playing hopscotch, actually: it is the interesting act of tossing a stone, hitting the next number and then jumping without stepping on the line. Each move forward made the job all the more perplexing, even while the basic route was well mapped out.

"It is easier to write a new book," I wailed to Susan and Mitch at AltaMira Press. "I have all this new material, and I am not the same person I was when I wrote the book long ago." "Add," they said. But which and what? Each addition causes other revisions, so in the end I cannot be sure what is original material, what is new.

So this book hops forward from old chapter 1 to a new coda, and back and forth it goes. Some of the new material comes from my experiences over the past twenty years, some from the way in which local history has blossomed and flourished, and some of the new parts are expansions of *History News* editorials that I have been privileged to write since 1995. Those essays appear here with the gracious permission of the American Association for State and Local History and editor Harry Klinkhamer. None is exactly as it was to begin with, as each has been tweaked in some way, usually by expansion.

What this book reflects now is my thinking about how and why we do local history, how local history has changed over the past quarter century, what doing local history means for our communities, what it means to us. This book is about the history of local history, the practice of history, the sources for local history, and its presentation. Some of the old chapters from the 1980s have been tossed in favor of more up-to-date themes, reflecting changes in the field and in my current thinking. Is this a revised book? Well, yes, almost all of the text has been reviewed and revived. Is it new? Well, parts of it certainly are. Whatever the publisher wants to call it is fine with me.

A great many people have helped me over the years, by allowing me to talk to them, to think aloud about the problems of doing local history, and inviting me into their historical societies to speak and offer suggestions. From the state of Washington, to Iowa, where I spent ten wonderful days touring and speaking for the Iowa Humanities Board, to Vermont, where I got to pull together thoughts about genealogy and local history, to the many historical societies where I have been invited to help design new pathways, I have learned a great deal. I am especially grateful for the long connection I have had with the fine staff at the Chemung County Historical Society in Elmira, New York, with the Upstate History Alliance and its director Linda Norris, with the kind folks in Cattaraugus County, and with my colleagues in Albany and around the state who are connected to each other on the New York History List. Susan and Robert Howard, editors of *Local History*, published in England, have become friends even though we have never met. I appreciate their response to what I have written.

I feel privileged, for, in general, local historians mostly remain embedded within the geographical confines of their own communities. While ranging widely across the country, I have met people who became friends and allies, and we have talked about the common themes and problems in presenting history. The Internet has also enriched my life, giving me a sense of community even while my own work has been locally based. There are many things I wish I had done, but I feel privileged to have had so many more opportunities than I could have envisioned.

I have a group of friends who have also helped, though they probably did not realize they were doing so at the time. Over the years, I have driven about or traveled from one place to another, and, with a captive audience, I have talked about the history of the places through which we passed, about the problems of doing history here or there, of the things that have happened. These friends, Jan, Elizabeth, Dorothy, Lauris, and some others, have listened and asked questions, and those questions have led me to new thoughts or insights. What we called "shopping trips" or "running away from home" were actually also local history journeys for me.

Staff members in Cornell University's History Department have been patient and kind—especially Kim Paschke, who wrestled with the problem of getting the text of the old *On Doing Local History* onto a computer disk through the oddities of scanning. My debts make me so aware of the kindness of the people in my life. At my side always has been my husband, Michael, who has aided me in so many ways, but mostly by being interested.

Introduction

This book originally began with some words about those of us who do local history. They seem apt still. *Amateur historians* too often *do* local history, or find themselves involved with local history, without considering just what history is all about. It is easy to accept local history as it has been done in the past—undefined, lacking in context, full of potential. Because history is in the public domain, because its content is frequently cited by a variety of people who are not historians, and because history is so often *used* by journalists, politicians, orators, preachers, and numerous others, history appears to be accessible to anyone with time and interest to invest. In this way, history is totally unlike the medical arts: medicine does not invite amateur participation, nor would the public long tolerate an amateur doctor or dentist. The past, however, belongs to us all; the language of history is the language we speak. Historical methods—except, perhaps, for recent forays by highly sophisticated historians into mathematical and statistical history—depend primarily on intelligence and common sense. Most history is not cloaked from view by an arcane jargon or methodology too complex for anyone who is interested to understand. Moreover, almost anyone can pick up a volume of history and profit by reading it. This very accessibility of the past permits anyone to become involved. Local history is, of course, the most accessible of all history, for it is closest to home.

A number of writers have set up formulas to be followed when writing, researching, or presenting local history: what to do and how to do it. Other writers have set down lists of rules for local historians, telling them—us—to write clearly, to use footnotes, to include maps. These writers address local history and local historians in a prescriptive fashion, believing it their duty to dictate steps to follow, to present a guide showing how history ought to be done. All of this literature is helpful, one way or another. What is lacking in those books and articles is the essential issue of thinking about local history, taking the time to consider what one does and why and what local history in all its forms means to the historian, to the public, and to our sense of who we are.

This book in no way duplicates those other efforts; these essays do not present, much less dictate, a plan for success. Rather, they attempt to consider what it is we do and the conditions and traditions under which we labor—amateurs in a field of endeavor in which there are highly trained and talented professionals who have developed a variety of sophisticated methodologies.

The word *amateur* itself has in our time come to mean one whose performance is less than the very best. "It was an amateur effort," some might say after a poorly produced play; or "Not bad—for an amateur," meaning that excellence was never to be expected in the first place. The word *amateur* comes, however, from the Latin *amator*, meaning "to love." An amateur historian loves history, both the past itself and the study of the past. Such a person tends to be known as a "history buff"—not one who runs about clothed in nothing but historical knowledge but, rather, one who buffs up, polishes up, reads up on historical events. If the individual specializes, then he or she might be known as a "railroad buff." An amateur who wants to know about the past of a particular area is called, for better or worse, a "local historian" or sometimes a "little old lady in tennis shoes." Amateur ornithologists—bird-watchers—and others share this appellation with us, but most often "little old lady in tennis shoes" means a local historian—be that person a male or female, old or not. The phrase annoys many people, as does the word *amateur*. The English journal published by the British Association for Local History even changed its name in 1968 from *The Amateur Historian* to *The Local Historian*.[1]

A number of scholars have written about the word *amateur* and about amateur status. Jacob Burckhardt, the great Swiss historian, commented that the meaning of the word had been spoiled because of the arts: artists must be either masters or else nothing; and they must dedicate their lives to art, for the arts demand perfection. Edward Shils, an American sociologist, cautions that "to be an amateur is a derogatory status. It is more acceptable among the rich to be an idler with inherited wealth than it is to be a serious intellectual amateur." Shils believes that, because of this attitude, anyone who is seriously involved with the pursuit of knowledge seeks the shelter of the academy.[2] As we progress through these essays, I think that we can substitute "professional organization" for "academy," because historians of all sorts who find themselves doing history outside of a university setting customarily seek affiliation within some organizational framework.[3]

Some complain that grants, prizes, and recognition are all geared to the academic historian, whereas amateurs suffer from a poor image, have difficulty getting their work published, and lack opportunities that are routine for those in the universities.[4] Life for academic historians is not quite so rosy as this suggests: some professional historians have trouble getting published, and all are not lavished with grants and awards. Other historians find themselves outside an academic setting by personal choice or because of the tight job market. We find highly trained historians working in publishing, at historical associations, and as historians in government or business.

In a somewhat gentler tone, D. G. Edwards, writing in *The Local Historian*, also tackles the distinction between amateur and professional. In answer to the question "Who is the amateur and who the professional?" he writes: "I would suggest that the only basic difference is that the latter makes a career of the subject and has been specifically trained for it. The good amateur must be just as 'professional' in his approach—he has to be critical, analytical, and imaginative."[5] I do not expect this book to alter the status of the amateur historian; but in it I intend to discuss why this situation exists, some of the ways we local historians might improve our image, and how we communicate local history to the public.

To begin, let me venture a definition of local history, for local history lends itself to many interpretations. My preference is for a descriptive phrase that allows for flexibility. I take issue with the outmoded English view that local history is the study of the origin, growth, and decline of communities. Promoted in the late 1950s and 1960s by English scholars associated with Leicester University, this definition confines one to identifying a particular community and then following a narrow course to determine its past. Nor do I believe that local history is only national history writ small, for such a view would place me in the position of looking only for that which can be found in the larger historical picture while ignoring the special rhythms and themes that emerge in my particular locale.

I see local history as the study of past events, or of people or groups, in a given geographic area—a study based on a wide variety of documentary evidence and placed in a comparative context that should be both regional and national. Such study ought to be accomplished by a historian using methods appropriate to the topic under consideration while following general rules of historical inquiry: open-mindedness, honesty, accountability, and accuracy. This definition legitimizes all sorts of research projects. Local history is, at its heart—as is history itself—the study of the human condition in and through time. We look for an understanding of our past. If that past is relevant to understanding our present or future condition, then that is all to the good, but this need not be our only goal. Doing local history is a process of learning, and it is about explaining causes—the how, and the why, of the past.

Local history is, despite its limited geographical focus, a broad field of inquiry: it is the political, social, and economic history of a community and its religious and intellectual history too. It is a place to look for individual reactions to historical events and the arena in which to practice demographic investigation. Local history is the place to hear women's voices, find information about child-rearing practices, ask questions related to education, leisure, and privacy. Local history allows us to look at town planning and our domestic architecture. It begs for studies of how we have lived in the past, in this particular place, and it offers an opportunity to study group biography, leadership, philanthropy, crime, and gender. Local history is the study of who remained in a community and who left—and why.

Local history is the framework in which to practice cultural history in an attempt to understand an area's distinctive style. The local historian has, in addition to documents, objects that add material culture to the historian's "bag of tricks": architecture, clothing, products of local manufacture, and the environment all become important. The tools and the products of folklore and folklife studies—sometimes confused with local history—can illuminate the story of local history. Local history encompasses many forms of history, and it uses a variety of historical methods—from oral to statistical to literary.

There is no standard apprenticeship that one must follow in order to research and write history. An artist, a master painter or one of the Sunday variety, must learn to mix colors, understand perspective, and think about selection—what to put in a painting and what to leave out. These same problems, or variations on them, occur in the historical context also, but few amateurs take the time to focus on anything but the immediate story to be told. Most amateurs become so engrossed with the job of research and the pleasure of writing up materials that they generally fail to identify questions that the discipline of history asks, much less discuss or consider appropriate ways of finding answers. Blame for this situation can easily be allocated. Many local historians fail to read historical literature from outside their own locales or areas of special interest. For example, one well-regarded local historian, in a small township located 20 miles away from a fair-sized American city, insists that a study of nineteenth-century religion in the nearby urban area is not of interest or importance to her own community. She cannot be moved to read the new book. This is not an extreme or uncommon situation, nor is the local historian involved a lazy woman. She simply does not see that the history of a nearby community may be relevant to the history of *her* community. She does not read history for ideas or for the methodology employed; she simply wants "to know" what happened in her community.

But! More blame than this remains to be distributed, for professional historians in the United States have almost totally ignored their responsibility to the amateurs who also labor in Clio's fields. With some exceptions, and until quite recently, professional historians have ignored local historians, have failed to share in the study of local history or to provide leadership, and have disparaged amateur efforts and most amateur activities. This situation is different in different parts of the country; some state historical associations have long been the meeting places for various types of historians, and some states have networks of local and professional historians that function on behalf of their areas' histories. With the advent of the Internet, there is even more possibility for engagement. Yet how many academic historians belong to the local historical societies in their own hometowns? More now, perhaps, than did several years ago, but unless they are brought in especially to help for a particular reason, many are disengaged from local groups. Academic historians have rarely taught, written for, or talked with amateurs. I can hear cries of protest from academe already. I know the many ways in which the local historian is vulnerable to honest and telling criticism. Still, rather than attempt to upgrade or improve, to encourage the work of local historians, by and large most professional historians have simply thrown up their hands and turned their backs. The responsibility that I am meting out belongs squarely in both camps.

Instead of rehashing old difficulties, I prefer to look forward, to attempt some mutual understanding—and ultimately cooperation—between amateur and professional historians. Since the 1960s, the nature of academic social history has changed. Local studies, using documentary materials in the community, are being pursued by graduate students everywhere. One result has been the publication of articles and books that should have import for and impact on amateur historians. This development has also meant that, for the first time in a great while, academic historians are coming into contact with local historians. More and more academic historians attend local history conferences as participants, more and more graduate students are seeking information in localities for theses, more and more people in general are using local historical resources. Will one group know what the other is doing or what its members are talking about? To help bridge this gap, some introspection on the part of local historians, about what *we* are doing and about the nature of local history, is necessary.

My purpose in this volume is to deal with the particular conditions under which a local historian labors and to raise some basic questions about historical method. I am interested in constraints on a local historian placed by documents, by society in general, by the particular local situation, and by the individual him- or herself. I will raise questions about various aspects of a local historian's activities: the use of evidence, the structure of research programs, language, relations with peers, the problems of audience expectations, and publication. This discussion is not only important for local historians; it is essential that it also occur in historical agencies when exhibits or new publications are considered.

My intention is not to tell anyone how to write local history, set up an exhibit, or put together an impeccable footnote, because books and pamphlets on these topics already exist.[6] Rather, I intend to identify problems that are particular to the field of local history and to open discussion of them. If local historians and those who run historical agencies recognize the complexities inherent in their work—if we appreciate the reasons for the existence of those problems—then we will become better, more thoughtful historians. I have a great many questions to raise and situations to sketch out; I have few hard and fast answers—although when I do have them, I tend to present them as though handed down by Clio herself. I have neither all the answers nor even all the questions.

Such a discussion for local historians has been attempted only infrequently. In 1943, John Caughey identified some occupational hazards faced by local historians—although by *local* Caughey really meant people interested in state history rather than researchers involved with the histories of their own communities.[7] Originally presented as a talk before the Pacific Coast

Branch of the American Historical Association, Caughey's essay appeared in the *Pacific Historical Review*. In 1967, H. P. R. Finberg, tongue in cheek, noted some sins commonly committed by local historians in a sprightly essay entitled "How Not to Write a Local History," which also originated as a lecture and was then published in a volume of essays.[8] I have borrowed freely from both articles, although neither man is an amateur local historian. Although each identifies important issues, neither hears the beat and rhythm of a local historian's experience. Neither scholar views problems from the vantage of an amateur who keeps his or her own community's past. Others too, more recently, have written about local history; they have been consulted and will be mentioned in the course of these essays.

Conditions differ in our field from state to state and from one area to another. Some local historians are aided in their work by active state historical societies that provide information and advice to individuals involved in local history. In other places, historians have banded together locally to talk about their activities and to learn from each other—often under the aegis of the state historical society. In many states, local history activities are carefully considered, whereas in other states, local history and local historians receive little encouragement—or help. Some local historians work alone. There is no way to speak to every situation. Because I work on the local history of my county and of my portion of New York State, many of the illustrations in this book are drawn from close to home. Although I have read widely in order to know what is current in many places, there is no way that I can be familiar with the specifics of local history everywhere. I believe, however, that the situations and conditions discussed here are representative of problems faced by local historians, even if the specifics differ from place to place. If circumstances discussed here seem unduly old-fashioned or musty, you ought to feel grateful; if what is depicted here is comparable to the situation you know, you might take comfort in the knowledge that other historians are struggling to solve some of the same problems. I do not believe we suffer more gracefully if we know that others confront the same difficulties, but I do think that we can learn from the experiences of others to improve our own working conditions. That is really what these essays are all about.

I have tried to formulate questions about the local historian's experience, to suggest areas where problems lurk, and to warn of frequently encountered pitfalls and common failings. I hope to stimulate discussion about the issues, not to dictate answers or propose rigid formulas. I do not intend, in citing specific examples, to disparage amateur local historians—for I am one myself—but, rather, to suggest how very easy it is to fall into bad habits. My goal is not to point an accusing finger but to point at ways that the practice of local history in the United States might be improved by those of us who so happily occupy our time with it.

One of the privileges of writing a book is being able to say thank you to the many people who have helped and encouraged my work. My husband Michael is an academic historian from whom I have learned a great deal; my colleagues in the Department of History at Cornell University are unfailingly helpful; Judy Burkhard, Katie Stevens, Kim Paschke, and Jennifer Evangelista never fail to come to my aid. I am fortunate, too, to know many of the reference librarians in Olin and Kroch Libraries at Cornell. These wonderful people answer questions in such a way that I forget that the questions themselves are sometimes poorly put. Terry Davis of the American Association for State and Local History has been supportive over the years as she has brought the association into a position of leadership. There have been three editors of *History News* who have welcomed my efforts and preserved me from my overenthusiasms. Thanking Deanna Kerrigan, Lauren Batte, and Harry Klinkhamer is a pleasure.

In addition, I have had the good fortune to have the support of Mitch Allen, publisher of AltaMira Press, and the aid and friendship of Susan Walters, editor at AltaMira. I am so appreciative to have these good people in my life.

Notes

1. *The Local Historian* is issued four times a year for the British Association for Local History by the National Council for Voluntary Organizations, 26 Bedford Square, London, WC1B H3U, England.

2. Jacob Burckhardt, *Reflections on History* (Indianapolis: Liberty Classics, 1979), 53–54; Edward Shils, "On the Spirit and Form of Our Intellectual Institutions," *Bulletin of the American Academy of Arts and Sciences* 40 (April 1982): 9.

3. *The Public Historian* was founded in the fall of 1978 in response to the needs of historians who function outside the academic world. This journal represents historians working in a variety of settings. It is published by the Graduate Program in Public Historical Studies, Department of History, University of California, Santa Barbara. Its first editor was G. Wesley Johnson Jr. Submissions are sought from "academic historians, public historians and other persons actively involved or concerned with historical research and interpretation in the community, government and private sectors." Manuscripts for *The Public Historian* may deal with various aspects of public history: commentaries that discuss and analyze various issues, methodologies, and professional matters pertaining to the field of public history and the work of public historians; research that uses historical methodology and perspective on matters concerning or benefiting community, government, and private sectors; or reports describing the specific work and occupation of a public historian or others performing historical research in the community, government, and private sectors.

4. Editor, "Soapbox," *CHAT (County Historians [of New York] Association Tidings)* (Rochester, New York), Summer 1978.

5. "From Readers," *The Local Historian* 9 (February 1971): 226–32.

6. Thomas Felt, *Researching, Writing, and Publishing Local History* (Nashville: American Association for State and Local History, 1976); Donald Dean Parker, *Local History: How to Gather It, Write It, and Publish It* (New York: Social Science Research Council, 1944).

7. John Caughey, "The Local Historian: His Occupational Hazards and Compensations," *Pacific Historical Review* 12 (March 1943): 1–9. Caughey's essay has been reprinted in *The Pursuit of Local History: Readings on Theory and Practice,* ed. Carol Kammen (Walnut Creek, Calif.: Alta-Mira Press, 1996), 200–8.

8. H. P. R. Finberg, "How Not to Write Local History," in *Local History: Objective and Pursuit,* H. P. R. Finberg and V. H. T. Skipp (Newton Abbott, England: David and Charles, 1967), 71–86 and in *The Pursuit of Local History,* 191–99. Finberg's essay "Local History" also appears in *Local History: Objective and Pursuit,* H. P. R. Finberg and V. H. T. Skipp (Newton Abbott, England: David and Charles, 1967), 25–44.

1

Local History's Past

Local history is not only a challenge to the most highly trained master of historical techniques; it is also—and long may it remain!—the last refuge of the non-specialist.

—H. P. R. Finberg, "Local History" (1962)[1]

Local history has long been with us, practiced at different times and places for various purposes. This is history that is sometimes clouded in myth, colored by forms of ancestor worship, or confused with ideas of patriotism or boosterism. It can be dated to the sixteenth century in England, especially to the frequently cited book by William Lambarde, *The Perambulation of Kent* (1656), and to approximately the same period in France. In both countries, it grew out of interest in nobility, castles, coinage, parishes, armorial bearings, and lineages. Some of the books produced were well done, if limited in outlook, whereas others were "mere vestiges of error, and some of fraud, which time and vanity had rendered sacred."[2] Most were written without plan, and whatever information was known about an area was included; whatever was distasteful or not of interest to the writer, or to the writer's aims and objectives, was ignored.

The pattern of writing history in the New World was little different from that in the Old. Writing history during America's colonial period was often stimulated by political motives, while some history was providential, "proving" God's will and America's unique mission. In the eighteenth century, history writing in the colonies tended to be colored by political views. Books stressed a provincial identity, often with an eye to encouraging immigration. After the American Revolution, history writing tended to justify the actions of Americans in the recent war, and it attempted to create a national myth. Although there were local histories right from the start in the eastern states, most attempts at writing the history of a particular community date from the 1840s for a good part of the nation, and from after the centennial in 1876 for just about every other place that was by then substantially settled. Hermann E. Ludewig, writing in 1846, noted: "No people in the world can have so great an interest in the history of their country, as that of the U.S. of North America: for there are none who enjoy an equally great share in their country's historical acts." He insisted that the history of the United States contains the "political and moral history of mankind, and it points to the way of greater perfection, which a free nation ought continually to strive to attain."[3]

By and large, writers of local histories prior to 1870 have been called by one scholar "patrician historians."[4] Although *patrician* might aptly describe some of these writers, many others among our nineteenth-century authors might better be called members of the nascent professional class whose occupations allowed them the leisure to engage in the writing of history. What these men—and they were nearly all men—had in common was some measure of education and an interest in writing essays about their hometowns. The newspaper publishers, editors, lawyers, doctors, and ministers who wrote much of the earliest nineteenth-century local history had some common concerns, and because they generally created the first—and sometimes the only—history of a community, their attitudes toward history writing influenced the writing of local history thereafter. Their style of writing and the topics they addressed shaped the public's idea of what local history is and how it should be presented. They created the patterns from which many local historians have only over the past twenty-five years freed themselves.

These early writers hoped to lure settlers to their communities. They promoted the healthy situation of their towns or counties, discounting reports of persistent problems, illness, or lack of opportunity. Many of their histories were commemorative—a memorial to or a remembrance of the early settlers. H. C. Goodwin, in 1859, wrote that "it is a duty which we of the present generation owe to the memory of the pioneers of civilization in the region of the country where we dwell, to gather up with care whatever records of the times there are left, and studying them well, transmit them in the most enduring form to successive ages."[5] And if Goodwin wrote because of a duty the present owed to the past, then Franklin B. Hough wrote because "there are certain duties which the Present owes to the Future, to transmit in a permanent form the record of the Past, that the memory of olden time, and the names of those who have aided in the formation of society fall not into oblivion."[6]

Some local histories were written to show the degree of culture to be found in an area, so that a community would not be written off as backward or regarded by its residents (or others) as a backwater. To this end, a number of authors produced promotional pamphlets in the guise of history. "The contrast," wrote one author in 1847, extolling the present state of his village as compared with its rude beginnings some fifty years earlier,

> is hardly to be comprehended. The change from toil, privation, and constant efforts to those of ease, repose, and tranquility; from the hardy pioneer's life, to one of affluence and splendor; from the rustic garb to the finer and most costly fabrics of American and English manufacture; from a dense wilderness, to rich, fertile fields; from low, filthy, and miasmatic lagoons, to dry, healthy, and beautiful flower gardens; from the absence of learning and literary pursuit, to the flooding of every species of intelligence.[7]

Progress was regarded, in this case, as change that improved life and eased toil. Change tended to be viewed as more ominous, however, when it brought about alterations in the character of the population or in the mores of a community. Progress could mean increase: from little to fulfillment, from overlooked to renown, from want to plenty. For those people who worked hard, it was the deserved and expected reward. Other changes were seen as destructive of old values when they created diversity of population or moved leadership from those people who had traditionally held power and influence to newcomers or those perceived to be outsiders.

The Fourth of July was an occasion when history was sometimes expounded in oral presentation. When public lectures became the vogue in our communities, the history of a town was considered a fitting topic. These orations frequently treated events as if chronology alone were history, yet the public found such recitations acceptable, and they tended, when published, to be popular souvenirs.[8] Putting a date on an event was deemed an appropriate historical activity.

Some histories were imitative or a form of competition, written because another community (particularly a neighbor or rival for population, manufacturing, or prestige) already had such a record. "That which suggested the present enterprise and which has resulted in the production of the following history," noted one author in 1840, was the reading of another town's book.[9] He then asserted that his community's history "would not be without interest even to the present generation." This last statement reveals another important motivation for the writing of local history. Local histories were often regarded as inspirational and instructional, especially to the youth of a community—those young people who took for granted and were perhaps even disenchanted with the opportunities to be found in the places where they lived. The unrelenting story in these "small histories" is of a hardy pioneer who moved to virgin land and, by dint of hard work and belief in the Christian religion, made for himself and his family the rosy existence that they presently enjoyed. The hardy pioneer's wife is rarely mentioned, but that is another problem altogether. These histories present a didactic lesson, even to the contemporary generation, and "cannot fail to be deeply interesting and instructive to the present inhabitants." Used extensively in the past, *virgin forest* is a term that today makes us wince.[10]

Some histories, like newspapers of the era, were forms of local boosterism, demonstrating that a small enclave was the center of all that was progressive and enterprising. In fact, these two words, *progress* and *enterprise*, recur over and over again in the descriptions of places about which our local historians wrote.

They were reflecting, of course, the very words that the settling generation used: the first steamboat on Cayuga Lake was called *The Enterprise.* Comparable examples abound.

These histories promoted a town, boosted its image, and attempted to demonstrate—especially to youth—that prosperity could be found at home. They also played on feelings of local pride and clannish associations. "Those who read this volume," stated one historian, "will find their fathers or ancestors, their relations or acquaintance," for the book was about the land of their nativity—or perhaps of their adoption, in which case their good sense was taken as approval of place and an indication of sensible choice. Such sentiments were important to cultivate, the same writer noted, "because it is upon the love of family and country, that all the social and virtuous affections are based." Ultimately, these histories represent a form of filiopietism, or local ancestor worship, of patriotism and attachment to the particular place where one belonged.[11]

George Callcott, writing in 1970, claimed that the pre–Civil War interest in local history "has never since been equaled." This, however, ignores the fact that the boom in local history really came after that war, when in 1876 President Ulysses S. Grant called on Americans to write the histories of their hometowns. Nor, writing in 1970, could Callcott know what was about to occur in the next three decades. He also observed that "the more geographically limited the interests of historians were, the more modest their accomplishments" and that town histories were written by a lot of "generally poor historians." Those histories with a broader geographic base, he claimed, tended to have a more lasting impact; for example, Timothy Flint and John Wesley Monette's histories of the Mississippi Valley or Henry Howe's historical collections of the West were more important, to Callcott, than town chronicles that were "generally detailed, highly factual, liberally sprinkled with genealogy, and frequently 700 pages or more in length."[12] Certainly it is true that a broader region requires the historian to see general patterns, to use material to support a larger theme, to explain rather than to recount. However, discounting the importance to their communities of even the more restricted histories should not be done lightly.

Local histories were often written to promote local and national heroes. Indeed, those books usually mention the major figures in a town's past, and certainly every "important figure"
who passed through the area is given his due. These histories do
more than promote public heroes, though. They tend, over time,
to democratize heroism: that is, they imply heroism in Everyman, or at least in every citizen of the community (excluding, of
course, African Americans, transients, women, and people
whose position was marginal, such as laborers and tenant farmers). Each settler mentioned in local history was someone who
had selected that place, and each had built a life for himself and
his family that embodied outward, or public, satisfaction. Those
who did not succeed, or did not remain, were omitted from the
history, many because they were not seen as important to the life
of the community and others because they lacked the funds to
pay the subscription fees required for inclusion. Those men who
stayed in a community, appeared upstanding, and strove for material success, earthly rewards, and a Christian afterlife were seen
in heroic or at least historic proportions—something that had
been, in the past, reserved for a few, not available to "almost any
man." The success of the early settlers, said one author, "induced
many to look with desire" toward this country. Where history in
Europe concentrated on the church and the manor, the priest and
the lord, local history in the United States extolled the successful
businessman, the upstanding farmer. If this sounds rather like
Thomas Jefferson's yeoman farmer, the backbone of a republican
society, it is no accident.[13]

Jefferson's views were known to most of the writers of our
mid-nineteenth-century local histories, but so were the opin-
ions, styles of writing, and literary conventions of classical historians. Many educated American males—the patrician or
leisured historians—knew Latin and Greek or read the ancients
in translation; in the examples given in their histories and in the
language patterns with which they wrote, we can hear classical
authors echo through our own American setting.

Washington Irving laid out his debt to and knowledge of the
classic historical tradition in his *Knickerbocker's History of New
York.* He stated that, like Herodotus, who lacked written records,

he endeavored to "continue the chain of history by well authenticated traditions"; that, like Xenophon, he maintained the utmost impartiality and the strictest adherence to truth; and that, as in the manner of Sallust, he enriched his history with portraits of "ancient worthies," drawn at full length and faithfully colored. Thucydides had taught him to season his history with political speculations; but, as did Tacitus, Irving sweetened that which he wrote with the "graces of sentiment" and infused the whole with the "dignity, grandeur and magnificence of Livy." Finally, he had, like Polybius, sought to make out of the disparate facts that came to hand a history that had unity.[14] Washington Irving's history of Manhattan is satirical in tone, intended to amuse the public and to sell books. It is a literary tour de force, written pen in cheek. Most other local historians took themselves and their histories rather more seriously, expecting somewhat less of a monetary return.

Local history became popular in the centennial era spurred on by President Ulysses S. Grant's call to Americans to write the histories of their localities. The nation was seen as the sum of its parts. Literacy was on the rise, and for some people there was increased leisure time and a great interest in self-improvement, one route to which was history.

While the centennial in 1876 contributed to the explosion of interest in the writing of local history, other things, too, spurred interest in the field. The historian John Higham has pointed out that during the nineteenth century "the study of history in various forms . . . superseded the study of the classics as the chief vehicle for enabling man to know himself."[15] This shift from the classics to history can be seen throughout the century. One writer of local history noted that there are two sources of information—philosophy and history. The former addresses itself to understanding, whereas history enhances understanding and the imagination and wakens the sympathies of the heart. Of the two, history, he wrote, is the more important. Having minimized philosophy, the author looks more closely at history and poses a new dilemma for himself. He recognizes the study of antiquity as the greatest subject of history. How can he then reconcile the values of antiquity with the fact that the work he is presenting to the public is one of American local history—a subject barely two generations old? Easily done, purrs our clever author: the antiquity of the world is the story of its creation and of the people of ancient civilizations. So, too, the antiquity of the author's section of America is told as the story of its creation by means of its era of settlement and of the valiant pioneers who struggled to make it home. Although that settlement took place only fifty years earlier, he argues, it still had all the charm "as it would have if it had taken [place] five hundred years ago!"[16]

There are some less attractive reasons, too, for why people turned to local history during this period. The last twenty years of the nineteenth century was an era of increased immigration to the United States by people whose ethnic diversity challenged the hegemony of native-born Americans; it was a time when class divisions became apparent, when political disillusionment, fear of the unruly, and labor unrest swept the nation. Few of these aspects of the times were treated by the local historical societies forming at the time, for those associations became the refuge of people who felt beleaguered by change and who feared that their way of life would not survive the onslaught. Local histories recalled old times; they chronicled the genesis of a community, its first settlers, its prominent citizens, and the values they shared. Local histories presented a history of steady progression from rude beginnings to a contemporary civilized state, with home, family, patriotism, hard work, and Christianity brought along intact "to illustrate the privations, virtues, piety, patriotism, and enterprise of her people," as one history of a New York community states.[17] All the while, the treatment accorded to the pioneers of a community became a sanctified litany, a legacy that remains with us today.

Other motives offered by writers of local histories near the end of the nineteenth century include a desire to "rescue materials from fast-gathering oblivion" and a concern to collect the memories of older persons who could themselves tell what had happened or who could remember stories told to them of the earliest days of a community. Some writers wanted to "correct many errors" in past historical accounts and to "correctly narrate these important historical events."[18]

Gilbert W. Hazeltine's preface to his *The Early History of the Town of Ellicott*, in Chatauqua County, New York, sums up the motivations and style of many of these nineteenth-century gentleman writers. Hazeltine was a local doctor, and his preface, while lengthy, is so exemplary that it deserves our attention:

What is the *ratio justifica* of this book? Simply this. Our friends desired us to write it, and we wrote it; the Journal Printing Company printed it, and Merz put on the covers. It is a home-made book for home use; and the critics, if any, we expect to be to the manor born.

Our friends will justify themselves by saying,- "we desired to rescue the memory of our grandfathers and our grandmothers, and our parents, from the deep pall of oblivion which was fast settling down upon them—and the history of their homes in the wilderness, in which they labored so hard to secure blessings which we alone have lived, to reap and to enjoy. The hardy, generous, and in many instances gifted men and women, who lived and labored in what are now our busy streets, have left enduring monuments of their united labor, but the records of their individual selves, have been meager and unsatisfactory. The records imprinted on the memories of a few yet living—whose boyhood days were spent in Jamestown, before it had become an incorporated village, have been found, of all remaining sources of information, the most reliable and satisfactory. There are still living here a number of persons who became citizens from 1825 to 1835, whose memory of events has yielded material assistance by sustaining and strengthening the memory of the writer,—by what they themselves knew of, and had frequently heard related, of the early settlers. As the years roll on, their deeds would soon have been forgotten, if the extended sketches we have caused to be made by one who was an onlooker, had not been written and given to the world." This is the answer you elicit from our friends.

It has been our attempt to record the names and the deeds of the fathers, surrounded by all that constituted their homes—as we once saw them, and as, to-day, they are vividly depicted in our memory. We have labored to place before you, their children and successors—pictures of their persons,—their homes,—and their surroundings in the long ago when Jamestown was a hamlet in the wilderness—when the Pearl

City was the Rapids—when instead of the busy hum of a hundred factories and a thousand industries, and a city of comfortable homes and palace residences there were a few lowly dwellings, and the hum was of the saw mill and the busy boatman by day, and the howl of the wolf or the scream of the wild cat in the Big Fly, by night. The homes, the industries, the scenes here depicted, were to our noble but humble-minded fathers the all of human life—they bounded the horizon of their being—they were the environments of their existence. Memory had embalmed them in the hearts of their children, now few remaining, old and fast passing away. What is known of these Pioneers among the children's children, the present generation, is weak and shadowy, and is yearly becoming more and more dim, and at the end of another decade—even within that short period—folk lore would have claimed the little remaining of the memory of the early settlers. We interpose this feeble book to prevent such a disaster. We present it as a rough monument to their memories—their homes—their deeds—their lives.

Although conscious that we have used every effort, which could be reasonably expected, to accurately describe the scenes and events herein depicted, yet the invariable experience of others should teach us not to claim entire exemption from those errors and imperfections always found in works of biography history. History has been defined [as] "An approximation towards truth: We cannot believe that this definition even approximates to a true one—nevertheless it may embody a shadow of a truth, for every thing human is marked by imperfections."[19]

In the 1880s, history emerged as a profession throughout the United States, and gentleman historians yielded to university professors for whom historical activity was not an avocation but a specialized career. These men made history an institutional product. David Van Tassel ends his book on the origins of the historical profession in the United States with the epitaph that by 1884 "the long age of the amateur historian had ended."[20] Yet, during this era, when departments of history were being instituted in American universities and young men were looking seriously at historical studies as a career, amateur local historians were not daunted—nor did they feel superfluous. At the outset, there was no intention to make a division between the two groups.

Quite the contrary. One of the most influential practitioners of history set out in a very different direction. Herbert Baxter Adams, after having studied for a Ph.D. in Heidelberg, Germany, went to Johns Hopkins University to teach when that institution opened in 1876. Adams had the title of fellow at Johns Hopkins, and he soon began leading a graduate seminar in history. He directed his history students to local topics while he himself prepared a paper on the role that Maryland's delegates had played in the Continental Congress—a paper that he delivered at a meeting of the Maryland Historical Society. Adams attempted to promote cooperation between "the local cultural establishment and the emerging professoriat."[21] He stressed the importance of publishing colonial documents, and he urged the state to provide funds so that those materials might be made available.

At the same time that Adams was promoting local studies, Charles Kendall Adams, president of Cornell University and a historian, suggested that a professional historical society be formed. Herbert Baxter Adams took the idea forward, and he shepherded the American Historical Association (AHA) into being. It was his intention that the new association include gentleman scholars as well as professionals and that the AHA would provide direction for local historical societies: "The implicit theory of the association was that the professors would lead and yet welcome and honor outstanding amateur historians and seek to coordinate efforts of the many local historical societies."[22]

It did not work out so smoothly, however, for the needs of the professionals and the amateurs did not easily dovetail, nor was one group willing to simply step aside while young men preached the new historical creed. One young professor complained in 1889: "There were more nobs than usual in attendance. . . . I am a little inclined to think the thing is getting into the hands of elderly swells who dabble in history."[23] The amateurs had their complaints, too. Edward Eggleston wrote that same year that the AHA "seems to be run in the interest of college professors only and to give those of us who are not of that clan the cold shoulder." With some exceptions, the amateurs gradually drifted away. In 1904, a Conference of State and Local Historical Societies was created, meeting in conjunction with the AHA but arranging its own agenda and program.[24]

The amateur historian was certainly eclipsed during these last years of the nineteenth century and in the early days of the twentieth, but by no means did the amateur disappear—a fact ignored in most of the literature concerning the development of historical writing in the United States. Rather, the amateurs persisted, and some continued to write very fine books indeed: Theodore Roosevelt, an accomplished amateur historian, was even made president of the AHA; and Franklin D. Roosevelt functioned for a time as the Hyde Park, New York, town historian. Amateurs continued the work of collecting, preserving, and writing local history. While academic historians tackled national issues, they tended to overlook the history of America's hometowns.

Throughout the country, local historical societies proliferated and pursued the collecting of documents and artifacts, and local historians produced local studies. Observing the academics, these local historians hoped that their work would be more complete and more accurate than previously written local histories and that they could rescue original materials and information otherwise apt to be lost or destroyed. However, these later authors submitted themselves to a degree of self-censorship of the topics they included in their histories in order—like their predecessors—to present a community's past in the most favorable light. One writer stressed that he wrote only of those events worthy of preservation, while another wanted to create a history "of which all citizens can be proud."[25]

During this era, while other occupations professionalized, the practitioners of local history began to change. Many of the patrician historians—our middle-class gentlemen of some education and local status—removed themselves from the writing of local history, taking up club membership, perhaps, and golf. The newcomers who moved into the field quickly demonstrated that writing local history was a challenge for them and that they were unaccustomed to or at least less than comfortable with the task. One author, Christfield Johnson, who wrote a centennial history of Erie County, New York, noted that his book had taken him fifteen months of continuous work. "Had I known," he complained, "the amount of labor involved, and the very poor pay to be obtained, it is doubtful whether I should have attempted the task." He also wrote: "If any one thinks it easy to harmonize and arrange the immense number of facts and dates here treated of, let him try to learn the precise circumstances regarding a single event, occurring twenty years ago, and he will soon find how widely authorities differ."[26]

Another author stated that his history had taken a quarter of a century to research and write. A third man complained that he had spent fourteen months writing his history. "I have been much puzzled," he wrote, "as to what to leave out. My promise was to make a book of 480 pages," but the completed book required well over 800. Arad Thomas protested that he was "not a professional book maker and has no hope of founding a literary reputation on this work," which he did not do. These complaints had never before been voiced by writers of community histories, some of whom were among America's most luminous literary men, such as Ralph Waldo Emerson. The earlier writers had the education to be comfortable with the task of writing and, with some surety, had picked their way through the tangle of information.[27]

The most significant stimuli to writers of local history at the end of the nineteenth century were the commercial publishers who hired authors, called compilers, to produce local histories. They believed that there was a substantial market for local history, despite the narrow geographical areas involved. These publishers counted on people being willing to pay to have a book containing the names and deeds—and, often, the pictures—of family and friends. The publishers devised a way of meeting their costs before they ever had books to offer for sale, and they thereby faced relatively little financial risk. Throughout the eastern United States there were a number of companies that kept their presses busy by turning out city and county histories. The books offered to the public were fat volumes, full of information and profusely illustrated. These books were not really written but, rather, compiled by agents of the publishing company with the aid of people in the community. Nor were these books really narrative history; they were collections of historical sketches, containing a great deal of historical information but little analysis.

If we look at the example of D. Mason and Company, of Syracuse, New York, we can begin to understand the scale of this new undertaking. Mason and Co. published seven New York county histories in seven years while simultaneously being involved with large histories of counties in Ohio and Pennsylvania. In 1884, for example, Mason hired H. P. Smith to compile a history of the City of Buffalo and Erie County. The next year, Smith put together a history of Cortland County, plus a volume on Broome County. Then he moved on. As Smith commented:

> It is the general plan of the publishers in the production of county histories to secure, as far as possible, local assistance in preparing the work, either as writers, or for the purpose of revising all manuscripts; the consequence being that the work bears a local character that could not otherwise be secured, and moreover, comes from the press far more complete and perfect than could possibly be the case were it entrusted entirely to the hands of a comparative stranger to the locality treated of.[28]

Neither Smith nor any of the other compilers who were hired to put together a history could possibly have written the story of a county in six months. Instead, a compiler would place a notice in a local newspaper to announce his intended project; then he would visit prominent people in the community to solicit their help. He gathered information, invited representatives of industries or individuals and those who knew about local institutions to write blurbs or donate material about themselves for inclusion, and offered them the opportunity to place their pictures in the book. Harold Nestler, who has studied and collected county histories for some time, cites the case of a man who paid W. W.

Munsell and Company, an Albany publisher, $150 to have his portrait and biography included in a county history. The subscriber received one copy of the book and twenty extra copies of the photograph. The going rate for such inclusions ranged from $50 to $300 an entry, and in this way the company recovered the cost of the book well ahead of its publication.[29]

Publishers advertised that the biographies included in county histories were representative of men of all professions: that is, that local history was eclectic, not elitist. In these books, we find portraits and biographies of upstanding farmers and businessmen, lawyers, self-made men, and descendants of early pioneer families who had come into the area with little and built comfortable lives for themselves. If each picture included in a county history cost $50, the lowest amount mentioned, then the publishers of an average book, with ninety-six images, could net $4,800 prior to publication. If, on the other hand, the average of the various forms of inclusion, from small portraits to a double-page spread showing house, barn, animals, and inset portraits of other family members, was $100, the publishers could amass, prior to the sales of the book, something in the neighborhood of $9,600. This sum would not cover the cost of publication of a large book today, although it would be an adequate amount of money, even now, with which to begin a project.

Why did people want to be included in such a volume, and at rates that can only be considered steep? What did inclusion in a county history mean to people who paid $100, $150, or more for the privilege? Obviously, one thing these people achieved was a form of immortality. In addition, they established themselves as solid, upstanding citizens, able to buy their way into such a book if they so desired. Thus the farmer with $150 to spend distanced himself from those who were simply eking out an existence on the soil or from those who had just arrived in the area and had no means to pay for space in such a book and had little stake in the community. The businessman, too, was able to show his worth, display his lineage, and purchase a form of everlasting advertising.

The history offered in these publishers' ventures was standardized fare, as the tables of contents testify. They were virtually interchangeable, and the biographical inclusions, whether the subject lived in Suffolk, St. Louis, or San Francisco, were much the same. Indiana folklorist Richard Dorson has pointed out that county histories from the northeast

> told one rigid, undeviating story. They began with a reference to Indians and the wilderness topography; hailed the first settlers; noted the first churches, the first schools, the first stores; devoted a chapter to the Revolution and the local "patriots"; swung into full stride with the establishment of the newspaper, the militia, the fire department, and the waterworks; rhapsodized about the fraternal lodges and civic organizations; recounted the prominent citizens of the community, and enumerated famous personages (chiefly Washington and Lafayette) who had passed through; listed a roster of the Civil War dead; and rounded off the saga with descriptions of the newest edifices on Main Street.[30]

The title of Washington Frothingham's history says it all. His book was called *History of Montgomery County [New York] Embracing Early Discoveries; The Advance of Civilization; The Labors and Triumphs of Sir William Johnson; The Inception of Development of Manufacturers; With Town and Local Records; Also Military Achievements of Montgomery Patriots.* This, historian Frothingham promised, was a history "of which all citizens could be proud."[31]

Women were the second group of people who moved into the world of the patrician historian. In 1883, the Association of Collegiate Alumnae suggested avenues of activity other than teaching that were appropriate for women, and local history was included among them. Prior to the 1880s, there were few local histories written by women. In New York State, of all the nineteenth-century histories I have surveyed, only two women authors can be counted; in Iowa, there was only one. *The Vermont Gazetteer,* created over the last half of the nineteenth century and edited by a woman, had but one woman author among all those who wrote town histories. David Russo, in his sweeping review of local history, found but two women in New England writing prior to the Civil War and few after that.[32] From the 1880s onward, although slowly at first, women could be found involving themselves with local history until eventually they became its primary keepers. It has been estimated that of the 1,600 local historians who today are listed by New York's State Department of Education, 80 percent are women, and most of them are over the age of fifty-five.[33]

In the past it was true that when women entered a field, be it teaching or typewriting, a devaluation of prestige and monetary return often followed. There was never much—if any—money to be made by local historians; local history would not derive esteem from the money it generated. Its regard came because of the connection local history made with place, with "old times and values," and because of the local status of its early practitioners. As most editors, publishers, and lawyers eased out of the field, the rising prestige of their own professions left with them—leaving commercial publishers, with their compilers, printers and pressmen, and women. Thus in the early years of the twentieth century, local history underwent something of a decline in prestige: feminized and commercialized. In addition, the errors of its past caused the public to regard it with less favor. Russel Headley, whose own work promised to "hue [*sic*] straight to the line," wrote in 1908: "It is a well-known fact that considerable prejudice exists among a great body of the people toward county histories in general, for the reason that some such compilations in the past, have been composed of fact and fiction so intermingled, as to render it a difficult matter to know what was true and what was false."[34]

Other significant factors were also at work to accelerate the decline of interest in local history. America was undergoing rapid change. The automobile altered transportation patterns and much, much more. World War I opened to Americans a vision of a life beyond the ocean; the 1920s roared for change and mocked the tyranny and mustiness of the past. Nothing could have been more old-fashioned, more passé, more out of date than local history. Malcolm Cowley complained in his memoir that education in his youth (circa 1916) was aimed at "destroying whatever roots

we had in the soil, toward eradicating our local and regional pe-
culiarities, toward making us homeless citizens." Cowley believed that only southerners retained any sense of place. "We
were divested of our pride," for students, he noted, studied every
history but that of where they were—a prejudice, he insisted, that
existed in public schools and in universities alike. George Callcott
noted, on the question of teaching local history, that "the subject
of local history was never really popular in the schools despite
state loyalty and even state laws."[35]

As widespread popular interest in local history dwindled,
most commercial publishers withdrew from the field. Getting local history published became a more difficult task. Historical societies sometimes picked up the cost, but more often an author
paid for the publication of his or her own book. These were ex-
pedients, however; the former perhaps more acceptable than the
latter. As one indication of this trend, J. Franklin Jameson wrote
James Truslow Adams about a woman from central New York
who had written him asking how to go about having a book of
local history published. Adams was at a loss for an answer: his
own first book had been privately printed, and his second, a history of Southampton, New York, was "brought out for his own
profit by the local printer who had printed the first one." Adams
cautioned that the locale of the history might make a book more
commercially acceptable. If, he suggested, the community is like
Concord, Massachusetts, with an interest in history and a built-
in tourist trade, the book might do well, and a publisher might
be found. For a less significant place, he had slim hopes.[36]

At this point we find yet another type of individual interested in
local history. Printers, pressmen, town clerks, and postal carriers,
during the 1920s and 1930s, began to put their names on books
and pamphlets of local history. I cannot document this trend
with absolute numbers, but I have collected the names and biographies of several of these individuals and have indications of
others. One was Uri Mulford, who in 1920 published lists of
marriages, births, deaths, and past events as a history of Corn-

ing, New York. In the introduction to this book, Mulford, whose education and position in society were far from those held by our patrician historians of the previous century, stated boldly:

> This book was written, the type set, the pages made ready for the press, and the printing done on his own press, by Uri Mulford. If I had not devoted a great deal of time during nearly a score of years, to research work, and had not purchased the printing equipment necessary to produce these pages, this unique, authentic and comprehensive history, *Pioneer Days and Later Times in Corning and Vicinity* could not by any possibility have been produced. The cost of production would have been prohibitive. The major factor in the success of the project, however, was my skill as a master printer—a craft that I have followed with minor periods of interruption for a full half-century.[37]

Another among this group of pressmen believed that footnotes impeded or intimidated the ordinary reader and refused to allow them in the pamphlets he produced. He wanted to entertain the public by using the materials of local history. He cared very much that people know about the history of the place where they lived, and he believed that it mattered not a whit if the stories were historically accurate or could be traced through scholarly apparatus. Another member of this group, when asked why he chased down bits of the past, replied that he was interested in preserving little items about common people "for Posterity."

"Does it really matter?" asked the reporter interviewing him.

He "looked genuinely surprised. He was silent for a moment, peering over his gold-rim glasses. 'Don't you think other people will enjoy it?'"[38]

Professional historians, of course, did not completely ignore local history. From time to time, the American Historical Association studied the issue of local history and debated the association's responsibility for and relationship to it. At its 1914 meeting, a committee of the Mississippi Valley Historical Association offered seven reasons why state universities should offer courses in state or local history. It was, according to the report, a state university's obligation to advance learning and promote culture; states owed something to history and were under an obligation to preserve their own; courses in state and local history were more appropriate for graduate than for undergraduate students because "other things than state and local history are more likely to be conducive to a student's culture, to his training, to his higher education." In addition, a state university should be ready and willing to lend aid and cooperation to the agencies within the state for promotion of public interest and knowledge concerning state history; the university should collect and publish materials pertaining to state history, and these activities should be under the auspices of departments of history; and—last but not least—research in state and local history was a rich field for graduate students as an exercise in how to do history, especially because local studies could be viewed as useful to national historians.[39]

A representative to the meeting from the University of North Dakota dissented. He noted that in many states, university people and historical society people did not come in contact: "In outer darkness are the people interested in state history." He also noted that professors of history would have to learn how to deal with people who carry history around in their heads, either as participants or as descendants. A professor would have to learn how to interview "to obtain valuable historical information" and professors would need to understand that "the folks will haze him if possible as being an easy mark." He did note that state history would guarantee a writer a large audience, although those most interested would be "the pioneers of the state" and probably not any others. The role of graduate students would be to gain access for the professor "to the people."[40]

It was in the public schools where local history was to be located. Beginning in the 1930s, and afterward, local history was often an option in senior high for students who needed extra credits or a local history project was sometimes proffered for students interested in history. As the years passed, however, local history descended into the grade schools, and for the most part, for the recent past, local history—if it has been in the schools at all—has been offered to fourth graders. The trend now, in the twenty-first century, however, is to abandon local history in favor of state history. The reason for this seems to be not that state history is more important or easier or even more appropriate for fourth-grade students but, rather, that state history can be tested by means of a statewide exam, whereas local history, it is generally believed, cannot.

During the twentieth century, local history acquired one of its most popular forms. Newspaper writers of the 1930s—and continuing to this day—seized on local events as interesting material for feature articles and weekly columns. Local history had appeared in newspapers before, of course, but mostly in the form of reminiscences, letters, and sometimes the results of interviews with aged or notable people. On occasion, a newspaper would publish a document that had surfaced, and, of course, newspapers noted the anniversaries of community institutions; of the founding of a town, business, church, school, or store; and of disasters—all of which sold well.

The appearance of local history in 1930s newspapers took a slightly new form, however. Journalists who reveled in an anecdote, a joke, or a regional dialect would take a story, polish it, and present it to the paper's readers. Their interest was in the telling of highly specific stories, which they did with verve. The demands that these journalists faced included the needs of editors to fill space with local, particular, "upbeat," hometown material; the pressures of a deadline; and the desire to amuse or entertain readers. Ultimately, these writers were trying to sell newspapers and maintain reader loyalty. Such newspaper writers were, and continue to be, very influential. They told pieces of a community's past in its most readily available form and in an entertaining fashion. Some of their stories are insightful—important additions to an area's knowledge of its own past—some are less so. The writers' purpose was to take local history out of the hands of those who had made it dull and wearisome, to democratize it, and eventually to commercialize it. As one of them wrote: "But what about the self-trumpeted historians who are determined to keep history for the few by locking it up except on appointed occasions or deliberately making it dull?" He stormed on: "A few of us are trying to make . . . history more alive than it was made for us." When asked whether his work was fact or fiction, he said he didn't care a whit so long as it was read. That, of course, is an entirely different object than the goal of most local historians.[41]

These writers were determined to inject some vitality into history, and they did. Their newspaper columns were popular then, and similar ones continue to be today. Not only did the public get a snappy story to accompany the news and sports, readers also acquired a notion of what local history could and should be. Local history was considered a source of local entertainment, as well as a source of local pride.

The ways of doing local history in the past have been as varied as the reasons for writing local history. Older histories established patterns that amateur historians and the public have accepted as suitable for the genre. W. G. Hoskins, an influential English historian, noted in 1967 that "in trying to guide local historians into the paths of righteousness and away from the amateurish imbecilities that often marked much of their work in the past, I am in danger of taking all the pleasure out of local history."[42] To change the format is often to lose the very people for whom one is writing; today newspaper writers presenting history in the popular press are among the few writing history today to attract a broad array of readers.

While the topics deemed suitable for history have broadened over the years, the topics ignored by local historians have remained fairly constant. Local historians have been, on the whole, antimodern and certainly antitechnological; they have been overly concerned with beginnings and with the distribution of land, without looking carefully at their own times. Local historians have rarely touched on topics that concern change, especially alterations brought about by technology, or ecological change, or the diversification of the population. As time has gone by, our local histories have repeated themselves—often to the point of reprinting earlier versions outright, without correction or addition. The table of contents of a local history published in 1950 is like one from the 1850s, with only a few new chapters added to account for the additional years. The outlook is similar from one century to the next, and the historical method used in 1950 was much the same as that used a century earlier. The motives of authors of local histories remained similar, too, and local histories at mid-twentieth century reflected historical patterns of the previous century, with little regard to advances or changes in historical linking and methodology.[43]

There were, however, significant developments in the historical profession, some of which began to make an impression on local historians. An early inroad into local history by academic historians began in the 1930s with the development of a subdiscipline called "urban history." Moving away from political and economic history on a national scale, some academic historians embarked on studies of America's urban centers. They looked at sources local historians had long used and others that local historians had neglected; and they produced studies that asked about change over time, that sought to identify the continuities that persisted despite a community's growth. Blake McKelvey's studies of Rochester are models of this genre. Constance McLaughlin Green, another urban historian, wrote as early as 1940 that history "from the bottom up" (her phrase) needed to look at various aspects of community life, to explain what happened (and where and when) as well as why. She complained that most of the local histories she had seen were written for community self-glorification, were antiquarian, lacked perspective, and were dull. She recommended that local historians study the field methods of the sociologist and read cultural anthropology in order to gain a broader understanding of history and historical methods. In 1940, Green called for studies of nondominant groups in a community, of class antagonisms, and of the emergence of social responsibility.[44] Such studies require careful use of historical documents, of course, and a respect for what emerges from them. Merle Curti commented that he saw the need

for cultural histories of communities: studies that would yield information about the backgrounds and education of settlers and later citizens; cleavages in communities and their various effects upon community institutions; the roles played by

church, school and press; the forces, too little studied, which
differentiate one community from another; and the relations of
Main Street to the world.

Curti also noted that "here the vigorous local interest that is
sometimes channeled into antiquarian backwaters can join deep
historical currents."[45]

The work of Green and Curti and other urban historians
(whose important research continues to this day) has had relatively little impact on local historians. One academic historian
told me recently that only three copies of his important, and frequently quoted, study of a community had been sold in that
place, yet it is now considered something of a classic and is read
by most graduate students in American history. Local historians
tend to continue in established patterns, their history rich with
detail, quaint ways, and sayings, their readers content. In 1950,
Richard Shryock noted that two types of historiography had developed in the United States. "The professionals," he wrote,
"were concerned with over-all developments and interpretations; the local historians with a summary of the facts." He observed that local historians tended to be interested in "everything which had happened just because it had happened."[46]

An institutional link between local historians and the history
professionals was formed with the birth, in 1940, of the American Association for State and Local History. That organization
has advanced the cause of local history and its practitioners in a
variety of ways, although its focus is more clearly on historical
organizations and their needs than on those who write local history. Today, the greatest potential bonds among the various
workers in Clio's field are a new wave of interest in local historical studies on the part of academic historians and a new sense
of purpose among local historians. The "new" social history has
spread into many areas of academic historical work; its research
materials are to be found in America's localities, and it has the
potential to interest both groups of historians. Its researchers
turn to local archives and to questions of a demographic nature
in order to know the past more fully. New studies of mobility, religion, population, race, gender, class, and family life have

opened up new historical questions and exciting ways of seeking answers.[47]

This "new" social history did not spring into being without antecedents. Its origins can be found in the work of American urban historians and among historians abroad. In England, academic interest in local history in the later 1950s culminated with the establishment at the University of Leicester of a Chair of English Local History. Interested in the origin, rise, and decline of communities, the Leicester School sought to encourage careful, thoughtful work by amateurs and professionals alike. Today, British social historians have expanded on the outlook of the Leicester School and embarked on broader demographic studies of English life in the past. Local history is taught in a number of colleges, and there are two local history journals that address the needs and concerns of amateur historians.[48]

In France, the route to local history came in the form of demographic studies rooted in department, or provincial, records. Researchers sought the answers to questions of national importance in local archives. Local history alone, the great French historian Marc Bloch said, "makes the study of more general problems possible." Wedded to this use of sources in villages and in departmental archives was the quest for knowledge about all of society, not merely information about those people who traditionally had power and whose history has generally been written. This was history that built carefully from an economic understanding of village life to look at all the people in the area, their system of work, and ultimately their culture. In addition, French historians attempted to understand long-range trends in population change—trends that were probably unperceived even by the participants themselves. These gigantic studies were ultimately made possible by limiting the area in which the researcher worked: that is, the geographic area of the study put reasonable limits on questions about the nature of life in the past. The computer became the technological assistant that made it possible to deal with such vast quantities of material in new and sophisticated ways. New and interesting historical studies continue to provide models. For example, *Enduring Memory: Time and History in a French Village* by Françoise Zonabend focuses on the rituals and patterns of daily life and has a great deal to teach American local historians by suggesting new topics and methods of doing local history.[49]

In the United States, the "new" social history borrowed from these foreign trends and adapted them to the types of information and questions important in this country. During the 1970s and 1980s there was academic interest in local history, but that interest does not in any way account for local history's new popularity with the general public. In the 1970s the country experienced *Roots,* the *Foxfire* series of books that focused on traditional life and folkways, and the architectural preservation movement that touched so many of our cities and towns. In addition, the national celebration of the bicentennial of the American Revolution took place, in its most meaningful form, in America's hometowns. Just as during the period of the centennial celebration in 1876, the bicentennial stressed our hometown heritage, and with it came an outpouring of interest in local history. A new crop of books of local history emerged. Unfortunately, many were simply reprints of older, nineteenth-century histories, but some were new works of history written by local authors. A number of books also appeared that dealt with the doing of local history, and these proved to be popular with the public.

Over time, local history has formed, developed, re-formed, and come of age. Its past bequeathed certain patterns, and it took from each era characteristics that have marked it well. Over time, for many reasons, it moved from the shadows into a commanding position in many of our states and cities, counties and towns—the past twenty-five years and the time to come mark an especially potent time for those of us in the United States who do local history.

Notes

1. H. P. R. Finberg, "Local History," in *Approaches to History* (London: Routledge & Kegan Paul, 1962), 125.

2. Anthony Richard Wagner, *English Genealogy* (Oxford: Clarendon Press, 1972), 367; H. P. R. Finberg, "Local History," in *Approaches to History,* ed. H. P. R. Finberg (London: Routledge and Kegan Paul, 1962),

111–25; W. G. Hoskins, *Local History in England* (London: Longmans, 1959), especially chap. 2; W. R. Powell, "Local History in Theory and Practice," *Bulletin of the Institute of Historical Research* 31 (1958): 41–48; Pierre Goubert, "Local History," *Daedalus* 100 (winter 1971): 113–27. See also the Rev. Thomas Dunham Whitaker, *History and Antiquities of Craven*, 2d ed. (London: J. Nichols and Son, 1812), v, quoted in Wagner, *English Genealogy*, 381.

3. Hermann E. Ludewig, *The Literature of American Local History* (New York: privately printed, 1846), vii. David J. Russo has written an important account of the amateur writers of our country's history; see *Keepers of Our Past: Local Historical Writing in the United States, 1820s–1930s* (New York: Greenwood Press, 1988). Russo deals with the early antiquarians, the emergence of town and city historians, the formulas used by local historians, and the problem of local historians and academic practitioners of history.

4. John Higham, *The Reconstruction of American History* (New York: Harper and Brothers, 1962), 10–11. Not all these patrician historians were men. See Deborah Pitman Clifford, *The Passion of Abby Hemenway: Memory, Spirit, and the Making of History* (Montpelier: Vermont Historical Society, 2001).

5. H. C. Goodwin, *Pioneer History of Courtland County and the Border Wars of New York* (New York: A. B. Burdick Publisher, 1859), 94. See, especially, Russo, *Keepers of Our Past.* Russo worked from the Library of Congress local history collection to study the phasing of local history in the United States.

6. Franklin B. Hough, *History of Lewis County in the State of New York from the Beginning of Its Settlement to the Present Time* (Albany: Munsell and Rowland, 1860), 1.

7. Horace King, *Early History of Ithaca: A Lecture* (Ithaca: Mack Andrus and Co. Printers, 1847), 18.

8. Appleton Prentiss Clark Griffin, *Index of American Local History in Collections Published in 1890–95* (Boston: Carl H. Heintzemann, 1896), throughout; for almanacs and anniversary speeches, see Ludewig, *The Literature of American Local History*, especially 111–17. The term *oral history* was first used in Vermont in 1863 when Winslow Watson, speaking before the Vermont Historical Society, complained that much of the local history of the state was being lost as older residents who remembered it died. "I have been amazed," Watson declared, "by observing in my own local researches, the ravages made by a single decade among the fountains of oral history in a community" (in Clifford, *The Passion of Abby Hemenway*, 224).

9. J. Cooper, *The Chronicles of Cooperstown* (Cooperstown, N.Y.: H. E. Phinney, 1838); J. B. Wilkerson, *Annals of Binghamton* (Binghamton, N.Y.: Times Association, [1840] 1872), iii–iv.

10. Louis Bisceglia, "Writers of Small Histories: Local Historians in the United States and Britain," *The Local Historian* 14 (February 1980): 4–10. The term *small histories* originated with Dr. Samuel Johnson. See, too, John Delafield, "A General View and Agricultural Survey of the County of Seneca," *Transactions of the New York State Agricultural Society* 1850 X (1851): 397; and Nathaniel S. Prime, *History of Long Island from Its First Settlement to the Year 1845 with Special Reference to Its Ecclesiastical Concerns* (New York: R. Carter, 1845), 111.

11. Wilkerson, *Annals of Binghamton*, v.

12. George H. Callcott, *History in the United States 1800–1860: Its Practice and Purpose* (Baltimore: Johns Hopkins University Press, 1970), 87–88.

13. David D. Van Tassel, "Biography: The Creation of National Heroes, 1776–1849," in *Recording America's Past: An Interpretation of the Development of Historical Studies in America 1607–1884* (Chicago: University of Chicago Press, 1960), 66–67.

14. Washington Irving, *Knickerbocker's History of New York* (New York: G. P. Putnam's Sons, [1894] 1908), 1: 23–25.

15. John Higham, *Writing American History* (Bloomington: Indiana University Press, 1970), 5.

16. Wilkerson, *Annals of Binghamton*, iv.

17. Walter Muir Whitehill, *Independent Historical Societies* (Lunenburg, Vt.: Boston Athenaeum, 1962), 350; and Van Tassel, *Recording America's Past*, appendix, 181–90, in which there is a list of historical societies and the dates of their creation.

18. D. H. H., *History of Clinton and Franklin Counties* (Philadelphia: J. W. Lewis Co., 1880), preface; Nathan Bouton, *Festal Gatherings of the Early Settlers and Present Inhabitants of Virgil* (Dryden, N.Y.: A. M. Ford, 1878), 2: 1.

19. Gilbert W. Hazeltine, *The Early History of the Town of Ellicott, Chautauqua County, N.Y., Compiled Largely from the Personal Recollections of the Author* (Jamestown, N.Y.: Lewis Historical Publishing Co., 1887), v–vi. H. J. Swinney brought this particular history to my attention.

20. Higham, *The Reconstruction of American History*, 10–11; Van Tassel, "Denouement: The Triumph of National History, 1876–84," in *Recording America's Past*, 179.

21. John Higham, "Herbert Baxter Adams and the Study of Local History," *American Historical Review* 89 (December 1984): 1225–39.

22. Higham, "Herbert Baxter Adams and the Study of Local History," 1232.

23. J. Franklin Jameson to John Jameson, 5 January 1889, quoted in Higham, "Herbert Baxter Adams and the Study of Local History," 1232. And see Russo, *Keepers of Our Past*, chap. 12, "Amateurs and Academics," 191–204.

24. Edward Eggleston, quoted in Higham, "Herbert Baxter Adams and the Study of History," 1232; and Larry E. Tise, "State and Local History: A Future from the Past," *The Public Historian* 1 (summer 1979): 15.

25. George W. Cowles, *Landmarks of Wayne County, New York* (Syracuse: D. Mason and Co., 1895); Edgar C. Emerson, ed., *Our County and Its People: A Descriptive Work on Jefferson County, New York* (Boston: Boston History Co. Publishers, 1898), iii–v; Washington Frothingham, *History of Montgomery County, Embracing Early Discoveries . . .* (Syracuse: D. Mason and Co., 1892), 7.

26. Christfield Johnson, *Centennial History of Erie County, New York* (Buffalo: Mathews and Warren, 1876), 7.

27. Franklin B. Hough, *History of Lewis County, New York* (Syracuse: Mason and Co., 1883); John A. Haddock, *The Growth of a Century as Illustrated in the History of Jefferson County, New York, from 1793 to 1894* (Philadelphia: Sherman and Co., 1894); Arad Thomas, *Pioneer History of Orleans County, New York* (Albion, N.Y.: H. A. Bruner, Orleans Steam Press, 1871), iv–v.

28. H. P. Smith, *History of Cortland County, New York* (Syracuse: D. Mason and Co., 1885), 3. See Russo, *Keepers of Our Past*, chap. 9, "Local History as a Publishing Venture," 149–64.

29. Harold Nestler, *Bibliography of New York State Communities, Counties, Towns, Villages* (Port Washington, N.Y.: Ira J. Friedman, 1968), foreword.

30. Richard M. Dorson, *American Folklore and the Historian* (Chicago: University of Chicago Press, 1971), 149.

31. Washington Frothingham, *History of Montgomery County [New York] Embracing Early Discoveries; The Advance of Civilization; The Labors and Triumphs of Sir William Johnson; The Inception of Development of Manufacturers; With Town and Local Records; Also Military Achievements of Montgomery Patriots* (Syracuse, 1892), 7.

32. See Clifford, *The Passion of Abby Hemenway*, 95–96; and Russo, *Keepers of Our Past*, 27–28. For a history of British women writers of local history, see, too, Joan Thirsk, "Women Local and Family Historians," in *Oxford Companion to Local and Family History*, ed. David Hey (Oxford: Oxford University Press, 1996), 498–504.

33. Marion Talbot, "Report of the Association of Collegiate Alumnae," in *Worlds Congress of Representative Women*, ed. May Wright Sewall (Chicago: Rand, McNally and Co., 1894), 793. See also Joan J. Brumberg and Nancy Tomes, "Women in the Professions: A Research Agenda for American Historian," *Reviews in American History* 10 (June 1982): 285–86. In 1999 the acting New York State historian compiled a report entitled "Statistics from the 1998 Annual Report of the Local Government Historians of New York State," in which he found that of the historians who responded to the questionnaire, over 60 percent were women. It is unlikely that this figure has changed significantly.

34. Russel Headley, *History of Orange County, New York* (Middletown, N.Y.: Van Deusen and Elms, 1908), 5.

35. Malcolm Cowley, *Exile's Return: A Narrative of Ideas* (New York: W. W. Norton, 1934), 3, 31; Callcott, *History in the United States 1800–1860*, 90.

36. J. Franklin Jameson to James Truslow Adams, 1 March 1918, J. Franklin Jameson Papers, Box 46, Library of Congress; James Truslow Adams, letter to J. Franklin Jameson, 5 March 1918, J. Franklin Jameson Papers, Box 46, Library of Congress.

37. Uri Mulford, *Pioneer Days and Later Times in Corning and Vicinity, 1789–1920* (Corning, N.Y.: U. Mulford Publisher, 1920), preface.

38. See "Historian Man of Year," *The Ithaca Journal*, 2 January 1980. See also Helen Hooven Santmyer, *Ohio Town: A Portrait of Xenia* (New York: Harper and Row, 1984), 255–56.

39. "Meeting of the American Historical Association in Chicago," *American Historical Review* 20 (1915): 518–19.

40. "Meeting of the American Historical Association in Chicago," 518.

41. Henry Charlton Beck, *More Forgotten Towns of Southern New Jersey* (Rahway, N.J.: Quinn and Boden Co., 1936), 6.

42. W. G. Hoskins, *Fieldwork in Local History* (London: Faber and Faber, 1967).

43. John D. Haskell Jr., "Writings on Maine History: The Story up to Now," paper presented at a symposium on Maine history, Orono, Maine, 5 May 1978; R. Richard Wohl and A. Theodore Brown, "The Usable Past: A Study of Historical Traditions in Kansas City," *Huntington Library Quarterly* 23 (May 1960): 237–59, reprinted in *The Pursuit of Local History: Readings on Theory and Practice*, ed. Carol Kammen (Walnut Creek, Calif.: AltaMira Press, 1996), 145–63.

44. See Bruce M. Stave, *The Making of Urban History: Historiography through Oral History* (Beverly Hills: Sage Publications, 1977), especially

interviews with Blake McKelsey and Constance McLaughlin Green, 33–62, 203–344. See also Constance McLaughlin Green, "The Value of Local History," in *The Cultural Approach to History*, ed. Caroline F. Ware (New York: Columbia University Press, 1940), 275–90.

45. Merle Curti, in Theodore C. Blegan, *Grass Roots History* (Minneapolis: University of Minnesota Press, 1947), 247.

46. Whitfield J. Bell Jr., "The Amateur Historian," *New York History* 8 (July 1972): 265–82, reprinted in *The Pursuit of Local History*, 21–32; Richard Shryock, "Changing Perspectives in Local History," *New York History* 31 (July 1950): 243–60.

47. Lawrence Stone, "English and United States Local History," *Daedalus* 100 (winter 1971): 128–32.

48. Finberg, "Local History"; Powell, "Local History in Theory and Practice"; Alan Rogers, "The Study of Local History—Opinion and Practice 3. New Horizons in Local History," *The Local Historian* 12 (June 1976): 67–73; Hoskins, *Local History in England*; David Iredale, *Local History Research and Writing: A Manual for Local History Writers* (Leeds: Elmfield Press, 1974).

49. Marc Bloch, *The Ile-de-France: The Country around Paris* (Ithaca: Cornell University Press, 1971), 120; Goubert, "Local History," 113–27; Françoise Zonabend, *Enduring Memory: Time and History in a French Village*, trans. Anthony Forster (Manchester: Manchester University Press, 1984).

Coda to Chapter 1

Revising What Is Held as True

The artifacts of the past have a way of making us uncomfortable. We encounter in the local historical past evidence of other ways of thinking quite out of step with our own. In our concern for fairness and inclusion—some will call this political correctness, though I think it is not, at least, not exactly—these encounters may become problematic. We discover when we stop to read them that some of our historical markers are wrong, others skewed; that some place-names reflect the past as it used to be discussed, not as we today would prefer to discuss or think about it; and that public monuments reflect a particular, exclusive past without consideration of how others might view them. Sanford Levinson, in his book *Written in Stone: Public Monuments in Changing Societies* (Durham, N.C.: Duke University Press, 1998), discusses a number of interesting topics such as the Confederate generals who stride on horseback down Monument Avenue in Richmond, Virginia, a city with a large African American population; the Memorial to the Confederate Dead located on the statehouse grounds in Austin, Texas; and the Liberty Monument in New Orleans that recalls the 1874 takeover of the Louisiana government by members of the White League. These are but a few of the pieces of public statuary erected in one era that we today find inappropriate. Levinson quotes Kirk Savage: "A public monument represents a kind of collective recognition—in short, legitimacy—for the memory deposited there." Statues do not, he insists, "arise as if by natural law."

Levinson also discusses the present-day display of the Confederate flag, then flying over three statehouses.

Levinson's examples range from Eastern Europe, where regimes have changed public statues to suit the current climate, to the Shaw Memorial on Boston Common and the Suffrage Statue recently brought from the basement to the Rotunda of the Capitol. His concern, however, is primarily with the American South.

His book reminds me that those of us involved in local or regional history have relics from the past that also cause us difficulty. For example, we all recognize that there is bias in our archival holdings. Most of the records that were sought and collected, those that form the basis of local or regional collections and, indeed, most of what local history once was, stem from and document a community's elite—or its emerging elite: the commercially successful, the socially prominent, the upwardly mobile, those participating in community institutions. Most of the story is about the white upper classes.

So we consciously expand beyond this base, finding new ways to use the materials that are already in our collections and seeking additions to the archive of documents more representative of all the people of the past. Even old curmudgeons have changed their tune and cease to call that box of women's diaries "dull stuff." They have begun to regard it with something akin to appreciation, if not fondness. We find ways to overcome the problem of what the archive holds.

But still, local history, now and again, is apt to reach out and tweak us. Driving along a highway, we pass historical markers replete with messages that reflect a particular view of the past. Those markers were erected, for the most part, for centennial observations during the latter part of the nineteenth century or at the dawn of the age of automobile travel and the development of tourism during the first three decades of the twentieth. They reflect the historical concerns of those who had the interest and were in the best position to see that the markers were put in place. Thus, there is a bias toward old families or, in my part of the country, to families connected one way or another to the Daughters of the American Revolution who wrote the marker text and paid for the installations.

Newer highway markers reflect the historical fashions of our own time, so that, all over the country, we encounter monuments that reflect history's latest concerns, such as African American or women's history. This righting of the record reflects our need to be inclusive of aspects and people of the past once ignored.

Place-names, especially those of geographic features, can also bring us up short. This is true of Massacre Lake in Nevada and Massacre Rock in Idaho. Located along Interstate 15, Massacre Rock in Idaho commemorates an Indian raid made on passing emigrants in 1862. Well, we know now, from the work of a number of historians, that this might or might not have been what happened and that most "massacres" were hardly that. *Massacre,* of course, worries us because of how the word has been used to place blame on Native Americans for events that were usually pitched battles between adversaries. We recognize today that there is more than one way to look at a historical event.

Reversing how we think about an event or person of the past has always happened. Take the case of Mary Walker. Born in 1832 in Oswego County, New York, she attended local schools and then the Syracuse Medical College, graduating in 1855. She married, though she did not adopt her husband's name, and the couple practiced medicine together for several years until they separated. Dr. Walker had always been interested in dress reform; she wore the Bloomer outfit for a time and then settled into the habit of wearing men's clothing.

At the outbreak of the Civil War, Dr. Mary Walker appeared at a field hospital in Virginia and began to work. The Confederacy accused her of acting as a Union spy because of her many trips through the lines, and when captured she was sentenced to a term in the Richmond Prison. Upon her release, Dr. Walker continued to serve as a medical officer, even in the face of complaints by Union doctors who did not want to work alongside a woman. In 1865 she was awarded the Congressional Medal of Honor for Meritorious Service.

Yet in 1917 a federal board of review decided that the citation had been unwarranted and that claims of her heroism were untrue. Her medal was officially withdrawn and she died two years later. By 1982, however, the historical tide had changed again, and the U.S. Post Office issued a commemorative stamp honoring Dr. Mary Walker of Oswego. Her biography appears in *Notable American Women.* This is a woman about whom controversy swirled and whose reputation, both nationally and locally, shifted with the times.

What do we do about parts of the past that make us uncomfortable? We cannot always remove an offending historic marker from along a roadside—nor should we in many cases—but we can erect others to tell more of the story than the original offers. And we can make sure to explain to the public about the changing nature of historical interpretation, about the ideas that inform the history we present, and to stress, as Carl Becker did, that history is two things: it is the past, and it is what happens in the minds of historians who bring to the documents their own interests and concerns, as well as the interests, concerns, and historical understandings of their eras.

It seems to me that these debates about the past are one way of teaching a public used to thinking of history as static—having learned in school that history consists of right and wrong answers—that, in fact, what we know and how we understand depend very much upon who we are and on the times in which we live. As ideas change, so too do historical fashions—not in order to dress up the truth but to better understand it.

2

Thinking about History

I'm beginning to wonder should we trust historians at all!

—Hugh O'Neil, in Brian Friel's *Making History*[1]

Over the years, I have been very much influenced by three historians. What each has said about history has alerted me to problems, to situations that I have eventually encountered, and they have made me aware of the consequences of what I am doing, of what I might not have seen or understood left to my own resources. Each has aided me, though none of them is responsible for my failure to adhere to their high standards. Each has caused me to think more deeply about the consequences of a historian's actions. Two of these historians are dead; one is not, and he is my husband, so let's not deal with him: you should encounter his books on your own. The two who are dead are Carl Becker and Marc Bloch.

I could not have had better companions for the doing of history, and I would like to send you to their works: "Everyman His Own Historian," in Carl Becker's book of essays by the same name, and *The Historian's Craft* by Marc Bloch. Their messages stand up well over time.[2] Becker is well known to every American historian; he also wrote notable local history. Especially important is his essay entitled "Kansas" in *Everyman His Own Historian*, and there is also his book about New York politics in the period just prior to the revolutionary war. Marc Bloch, one of the founders of the French *Annales* School, was killed by the German SS in 1944. He wrote a book of local history called *Ile-de-France: The Country around Paris.*[3] Both of these men wrote with startling clarity about the craft of history; each knew what local history is all about, and each thought that local history could adhere to and represent the highest of historical standards. There are other historians I also admire, but I carry with me the words of these two. Each has written with a beauty that illuminates what he has to say. If you read Becker and Bloch, then you can skip this chapter. If you read them, and continue reading here, you will understand my debt to them and to others.

Carl Becker commented wisely that history is two things. History is the past itself—that is, the events that happened some time ago. But it is something else, he observed, for history is also what happens in the mind of the historian. Historians look for two things when contemplating the past: we look for that which has changed and that which has remained constant. A flood changes things; the river with its possibilities for good and harm remains constant. Town government is a constant; misuse of the town road fund is a point of change. When we identify change we ask a batch of questions: Why did this happen, how did the change come about, who or what triggered an event, what were the consequences of that change—on the subject itself or on parts of it, on those involved, on those watching from the sidelines? How did people react; what did they do differently; what did they miss?

If it is an institution under investigation, we must wonder why it has remained, what temptations or forces altered it or failed to do so, what sorts of things happened because of its constancy. A town board might be considered an example of an ongoing entity important for the governance it provides through the actions of those five or seven people who run the community and gain their position by election or appointment. The town board, however, also changes its functions as dictated by popular demand, by the availability of funds and their source, by state and federal mandate, and by the times in which it functions or that which the public needs or demands. So something continuous can also change over time.

If we look at something that changed—a local boundary moved, the switch of a church from one denomination to another, the failure of a company, or someone who acted and made a difference—in each case, the change occurred from within and from without, and the causes need to be explored. Yet, even with change, there are things that remain constant: the church continues to serve a congregation (although it might be a different group of people or even a different creed), the company might reorganize or be bought out by another. Individuals might become wealthy and therefore do things out of the ordinary, yet they will also remain themselves. We need to explore the role of the government, or company, or church— what precipitated change, what resisted change, and what forced the issue. Then we need to consider what the process of change was, how it was managed and who managed it, and what the costs were.

I am alert to change but wary too. I am always caught up short when someone says that the twentieth century dawned. Well yes, the date changed, but if what you mean by the twentieth century is modernization, a new age or scientific times, you will find that those things happened piecemeal, a bit here and something there, but not all at once everywhere or even anywhere. Finally, we need to wonder how that which was changed was different, how it fit into the local context, and who approved, who was alienated, and who benefited. We explore everything we can about the change from one status to another, always asking the paired questions: who approved, who didn't; who benefited, who didn't; who had influence, who didn't?

If we look for something that did not change over time, then we have to reason a bit more subtly. What does not change? Well, the land might be considered fairly constant, although over time our use of the land changes, the land itself can wear out, the ore underground can run out, or something can be found that no one previously knew was there. The weather, too, is always there, but we all know that there are weather patterns over a number of years, and so the weather changes. What else might not change? Well, for me the one thing that is constant is human nature. We learn more, we act differently in different times, but in so many ways human nature does not change all that much. We still have basic needs that can be identified now and in times past: we love, we create families, we are lonely, we sing and are happy, we have a need for belief in something—just what varies from person to person. We express anger, we are thoughtless, we covet, we are blind to much. On the other hand, we have, over time, become more tolerant of diversity, and if that is a facet of human nature, then even human nature changes. But Mother Love is a facet of human nature that remains constant, even while the definition of *love* and what it means in terms of caring for our young have changed from one period to another—just as the idea of who a mother is and what her role should be has changed.

What else might be constant? Well, over time we have formed local governments and we have created ways of trading goods, services, and money. We strive to be more than self-sufficient. We believe in education or improvement. So some things can be seen as the same, although they are altered by circumstances, by era, and possibly by place.

Carl Becker noted that while history is the past, it is also something else, and this is where we historians come into the picture. Becker said that history is also in the mind of the historian. What he meant is that coexisting with the past, with all its changes and constancy, there is also the history that is created in the mind. The historian, in an effort to understand the past, shapes the history of the subject in his or her mind.

It is easy to say, sure, okay, I know that. But Becker is subtle and wise. He is not only saying that we historians write the history of our communities; he is saying that we are creating the history of our communities in our minds. And he reminds us that the history I create in my mind is not, and can never be, quite the same as the history you create in yours. In other words, history is not a science that is replicable from one laboratory to another. History is not a formula to be tested that with each attempt will yield the same answer.

Recorded history is, rather, what happens in the mind of the historian, and this merits our attention because each mind is different. History is an art form, and it is important to remember that if history is in the mind of the historian, then it is subject to the interests, intelligence, and even the preoccupations and era of each individual historian. And where do those interests come from? Well, obviously, some come from our own inclinations—or prejudices. I do not do railroad history, for example. I just don't much care for train lines, and locomotive types, and car numbers. So given a batch of documents about a local train line—the DL&W (the Delaware Lackawanna and Western Railroad), for example—I will look at those papers differently from someone who wants to know developments in the type of locomotives in operation, how many cars there were, and their routes. I will look at railroad documents—if you can get me to look at them at all—in terms of what impact the railroad had on a community, who used it and for what, what happened before it was there, and what happened when the railroad company abandoned the route and the community. So this other "straw" historian and I would create in our minds, and on the page, two different histories even if we used the same file of papers. And the reason is that we are two different people with different interests and abilities.

So we have to ask again, where do our interests come from? Well, they come from a variety of things. My interests (and yours) come from our personalities, our background knowledge—other things we have read and have been influenced by. Our interests come from our abilities: if you can read Spanish, then you can use the material written in that language that may pertain to that railroad. Because I cannot read Spanish, I will not read those documents, or I will try to find someone to read and translate them for me. So right there our abilities have created differences in how we deal with the materials in front of us. If I can make neither heads nor tails of an account book, but you can, then you will use that material differently and most likely better than I. But because I am very sympathetic to workers, when we encounter them in a strike or in a library open to workers in the evening, I might reflect their past in a more empathetic way than you.

In addition to our interests, abilities, and personalities, we are influenced by our times. When I went to college there was no women's history. Well, that is inaccurate. There has always been women's history: it is just that, until the late 1960s, no one was looking for it, looking at it, or teaching it. Just so with black history: until the civil rights movement of the 1960s, only a few people were interested in pursuing the history of African Americans. So their history was not represented in our general history courses or even in specialized courses. Today, of course, everyone is interested in class, gender, and race, so these topics are better represented. And we think about them when contemplating a topic in our local history setting for an exhibit or publication or in thinking about how to approach a history topic.

Therefore, given those railroad documents we have been talking about, one person might be interested in where the trains ran and how often, whereas another local historian today might ask questions about who the workers on the train were—if all jobs on the railroad were open to everyone who looked for work or if employment was segregated by race and gender. The times influence what we are interested in, and they influence the questions we ask about the past, just as our personalities and our interests also influence the subjects we pursue in the past.

There are problems with documents too. Events in the past were just that. They were things that happened, they were life itself—they were not designed to be the subject of future research. All the documents we might hope to find about an event will not be there, and some of our questions about the past can never be answered. This is one way that the recorded past warps our present-day understanding. It happens in other ways too, for not all the documents created about an event may have survived, and this creates a skewed version of the past. Some of us, in addition, are better researchers than others—some are more persistent, range more widely, find ways of teasing information from sources; and so each of us gathers what there is of a past event in a different fashion. I might have a few documents; you might have many more. That difference will create different histories right there. But even if we each have identical documents in front of us, we will arrange them differently. If you and I have four documents about this awful train subject, I might ignore the account book, and you might use it; I might think the complaint by a widow whose husband was a railroad worker important, and you might not. We will arrange the sources we find in a different order, give different emphases to one thing or another, but in general, not to the same thing. And even if we both rate one document to be of the greatest importance, because we are different individuals with different skills, interests, prejudices, and training, we will not necessarily interpret that document the same way. When we think of the questions we want to ask of the documents, you and I will ask different questions; when it comes to writing about the episode, your ability to write well and my less able writing will further differentiate between the histories that we two will create.

Our sources present us with problems because not every document that might have been created was created and not every document has survived. As researchers we find different items to use for the history we are writing. So how we select the documents, how we arrange them, how we address them, and how well we think and write will also cause us, or allow us, to write different histories. "Do we need three hundred biographies of Abraham Lincoln?" a student asked me the other day, and I responded, "Of course." Each is different; each has a different focus; each represents a different historian's view and ability to create a Lincoln biography.

These individual differences in who we are and the times in which we work color the very topics we address, the sources we search for and locate, and what we make of them. In his play *Making History*, Brian Friel has Peter Lombard, the titular bishop of Armagh and primate of All Ireland, respond to the question "Don't you believe in the truth, Archbishop?" by saying:

> I don't believe that a period of history—a given space of time—my life—your life—that it contains within it one "true" interpretation just waiting to be mined. But I do believe that it may contain within it several possible narratives: the life of Hugh O'Neill can be told in many different ways. And those ways are determined by the needs and the demands and the expectations

of different people and different eras. What do they want to hear? How do they want it told? So that in a sense I am not altogether my own man, Hugh. To an extent I simply fulfill the needs, satisfy the expectation—don't I?[4]

Yet history does not change. That is, all the stuff of history that has survived is always there. It is our ideas about history that change; our ideas about what is important change, our ideas of what should be taught and known change, as do our ideas about what to look for and even how we pose questions about the past.

This is something that puzzles those people who went through school, taking history courses because they had to. Whether they enjoyed the subject or not, they learned that history is full of dates that needed to be memorized and then spouted out on standardized tests. For many of them, history is something with prescribed answers. Those people, because they have not had the chance to think more about history—or have not been challenged to think about it—are uncomfortable with the idea that history is not a set piece, that facts can be used differently, and that interpretations of history can see and reveal things where they were not seen or understood before. When the curators at the Smithsonian Museum on the Mall in Washington, D.C., wanted to create an exhibit about the *Enola Gay* and the end of World War II, controversy erupted. Many people, especially those who had fought in the war or lived through it at home, thought of the war one way. Historians, on the other hand, had seen new materials from the era, and they were asking new questions that caused them to regard the *Enola Gay* as a more complicated issue, not merely as an airplane that delivered the atomic bomb that brought about the end of fighting in the Pacific. In the fifty years since the bomb was used, public attitudes have changed too. But for some of the people, those who remembered with great relief that the war had ended, or for those in harm's way, for those worried about loved ones, ending the war any way possible was what was important at the time. They are, in general, not interested in different interpretations of something they knew and suffered through. To them, to consider other viewpoints is to deny the history they hold to, the history that they lived through and consider themselves to be witnesses to and authorities on. Who are the historians who can shake that firsthand knowledge? Yet the memory they hold to is but one version of the past, incomplete then and incomplete now: skewed.

And there are still other problems in doing local history. Those documents that we rely on to tell us what happened in the past were not intended to be documents. Rather, they were letters or diaries, memoirs, or business papers or accounts. We turn them into documents when we rescue and then use them, and then we worry that they do not tell us enough. They were not, however, intended to "explain" the past to us. We have turned them from their original function to our own purposes.

There is a problem, too, when local historians look only at their own communities and see events as unique when they are not; they fail to see that some things are common to a region or a nation. Indeed, many local historians fail to see whether materials about a community or about an event in a community's past might not exist in a nearby archive. This causes some local historians to limit what is available to them by failing to think within a regional scope. If one researches the effects of the Great Depression in Groton, it would be smart to see what was happening in Lansing to the west and Cortland to the east. Seeing what was happening in adjacent towns gives the historian a basis for comparison. Thus it is important that a community historian read the histories of nearby communities: sometimes pictures in common will appear that will enrich their work; sometimes it will become apparent that an event *is* unique; sometimes there will be illuminating comments to be found in neighboring places. We need to remember that though we might say we are doing the history of the Town of Caroline, people did not live their lives that way. Those in Caroline had relatives and friends elsewhere with whom they corresponded, who visited them, and who joined in their moments of celebration and sadness. The patterns of life were not lived according to geographic boundaries; neither should our histories be so limited.

There is a bias, in addition, in what paper and artifacts of the past were collected and preserved. Much of what has ended up in our historical societies and local archives has gotten there by chance—or by the idea that certain things are properly kept by a historical society. So the letters of a prominent family might be held in a local archive while the letters of a laborer in a tannery were not thought about or considered important enough to collect. Most local historical societies have accepted whatever was offered them, and what was offered was usually given by people connected with the historical society or with prominent families in the community. Thus the diary of a workingwoman might not have made it into the local archive and was not, until recently, even sought. The same is true of materials generated by African Americans, whose letters, diaries, and newspapers are rarely to be found in local archives. And when materials concerning African Americans, or Irish immigrants, or tenant farmers did appear in the collections in a society, those collections often were not indexed to show their presence.

The caution we receive from Marc Bloch is somewhat different from Carl Becker's concerns. Bloch worried about our ability to understand the past. Be aware—not beware!—of the present, he said; be involved in your own times so that you will understand human nature, and knowing it in our time will aid in knowing it in the past. What he is warning us about is that too often the past is regarded as some golden age and its inhabitants, as giants of morality with clarity of action; whereas the past, in truth, was peopled by individuals whose motives were as varied as our own, whose devices were like ours. They need to be understood as human beings even when the documents fail to show them with their faults as well as their virtues. Knowing human nature today improves our understanding of the actions and motives of people in the past. Bloch cautions that the historian disinterested in his or her own era is most likely to become merely a useful antiquarian rather than a historian. This is something for us all to remember.

At this point you should be wondering whether we can do history at all. Or should we? With all these flaws in the documents, prejudices in ourselves and how we approach the past, in the topics we think are interesting, how can we even consider ourselves historians? Well, we can and we are. But we are better historians when we know our limitations, our interests, and our biases; when we think about the problem of materials that survive and those that do not; when we recognize that materials are as fragile in what they tell us as they are in their physical form—that they will not tell us everything, that we will have to approach them carefully, that we must seek out their biases as well as know our own, and that, in everything we do, there is a context that when sought will enrich our own work.

Being aware is what is important. We can then research broadly, consider all the angles, approach a topic from various viewpoints, tease out the meanings in the materials that come to us from the past. These are the cautions a local historian—any historian, actually—must live with. Being aware of them, we will be sensitive to the fragility of what we do. Our communities deserve no less from us.

Despite the problems and pitfalls we are likely to encounter, we conduct local history research because it is important. Some of us are curious and want to know about the places where we live. Others seek answers to contemporary problems by looking at the past: why streets bear the names they do, why the town acquired a certain reputation, how the community reacted to national events, where the people came from—or where those who were once here went and why. Some use local history to understand how a community functioned—the town board reacts to certain strains placed on it by citizens' expectations, state requirements, or the lure of federal money. Some people want to research their own families or homes. Others want to know how a club, factory, or religious body came to be and then threaded its way through the years to the present. Some people, of course, are "professionals"—trained to be community, or public, historians—and they set out to conduct their working lives in one or various localities, interpreting the history of an institution or a place. There are many reasons to become involved. Thoughtful historians of our communities are always needed.

Notes

1. Spoken by the character Hugh O'Neil in the play *Making History* by Brian Friel (London: Faber and Faber, 1989), 8.

2. Carl Becker, *Everyman His Own Historian: Essays on History and Politics* (New York: S. F. Crofts, 1935; and in paper, Chicago: Quadrangle Paperbacks, 1966); Marc Bloch, *The Historian's Craft* (New York: Knopf and Co., 1952) and *Ile-de-France: The Country around Paris* (Ithaca, N.Y.: Cornell University Press, 1971). See also the essays about local history in Carol Kammen, ed., *The Pursuit of Local History: Readings on Theory and Practice* (Walnut Creek, Calif.: AltaMira Press, 1996). In addition, see H. P. R. Finberg, ed., *Approaches to History* (London: Routledge and Kegan Paul, 1962), essays about history by a number of British historians.

3. See Carl Becker, *History of the Political Parties in the Province of New York, 1760–1776* (Madison: University of Wisconsin Press, 1909); and Marc Bloch, *Ile-de-France: The Country around Paris* (Ithaca: Cornell University Press, 1971).

4. Brian Friel, *Making History* (London: Faber and Faber, 1989), 15–16.

Coda to Chapter 2

Censorship

There has been a great deal of talk, and some anger, about history over the past few years. I am thinking of a number of instances when the interpretation of the past has mattered— mattered enough for the general public to become involved with what at other times might be considered mundane or professional problems normally left to historians and employees of historical agencies.

Specifically, I recall the cancellation of the Smithsonian exhibit commemorating the ending of World War II in the Pacific that was planned for the National Air and Space Museum in Washington, D.C. The exhibit came to be identified by the *Enola Gay*, the airplane that carried the atomic bomb. The issues raised by that exhibit are important to local historians and to local historical societies because they involve, on the one hand, professional expertise and, on the other, the public memory and a general desire that history validate and celebrate our national past. These are not necessarily similar views of history. The one seeks to know the past by study, by questioning, by looking at what was said at the time and what we know in all the days thereafter. The other seeks to have history affirm national ideals and to allow us to see ourselves in the past as acting for the best of reasons.

In the case of the Smithsonian exhibit these two views of the past clashed and the exhibit was canceled.[1] In effect, the portrayal by professional historians and museum personnel of the bombing of Japan came into conflict with individual memories of what Americans in the military and those at home were told at the time and with our general belief that we as a nation had acted from the best of motives. A former bombardier wrote angrily to tell me that the life span of tail gunners was short in the Pacific and that dropping the bomb most likely saved his life—as it probably did.

But that individual truth is no reason why we should not explore the bombing as a historical issue in order to see the many truths of the era—those things that knowledgeable people said and believed, what the public was told and believed, and also the military and statistical information available now but not generally known at the time. People with a vested interest in the era and with a personal belief in the nation's motives were able to censor the exhibit by exerting sufficient pressure to bring it to a halt.

Local historians also censor history. This self-censorship is important to recognize because it limits the topics that local historians select; it colors our outlook about the doing of local history for the communities in which we live; and it skews the sort of history that the local public expects and then gets from local historical societies and local historians.

What sort of censorship? you might ask. I offer here some anecdotal examples. A woman I knew told me that she would never look into the history of the failure of her local bank because members of the family responsible were still in the community. She did not want to disturb or embarrass them. In this case, she exercised local censorship in order to protect the living from an unpleasant past. In doing this, however, the historian was also denying the community an understanding of the role banks play in people's lives, how ordinary people reorder life when their savings disappear, and how a community acts to provide for those in great need. Would this historian, I wondered, be as careful to protect the owners of a failed supermarket who had relatively little social standing in the community or the owners of a railroad that abandoned the station, they being outside the community and relatively anonymous? The historian was willing to bypass an important local episode because it might cause people to think ill of prominent individuals. She surely could have handled the episode without pointing fingers but, rather, by looking at the bank's importance to the community and the consequences of failure. What she worried about, I am sure, is that even if the man guilty of running off with the funds were not named, people would still know, that they would remember on their own, that discussing the episode would "dredge it all up again."

Or was this historian protecting her ability to do local history locally? Local historians are dependent on the community for information and new materials. An "unreliable" local historian, one who embarrasses area residents or makes them uncomfortable, will soon find documents unavailable and people unwilling to cooperate. The public has certain expectations about local history, just as prominent people in the past often expected newspaper editors to protect the transgressions of their sons. "A local boy of good family," reads one newspaper notice in 1858, "fell into bad company when in town." To ignore local expectations can be a self-defeating scenario, for we must continue to live among those about whom, or for whom, we write.

Another form of local censorship involves what a historical society is willing to take on as an exhibit, program, or research topic. Some historical societies, conscious of the need for local support and contributions, are loath to touch subjects that might be seen as controversial. Local history, after all, is generally considered to be promotional of place. This censorship of presentation derives from the attitude that local history should be boosterish of—or be good for—the community. Our hometowns are avid consumers of local history because it is believed to have a positive influence on residents. In addition, local history helps provide tourist destinations—places such as cemeteries, record offices, and libraries that are visited and used by local and distant genealogists. Local history appears in the newspaper because it provides good "copy" or publicity about place.

A third variety of local censorship comes in the form of disappearing documents. A friend of mine, researching the lives of teenaged girls in the nineteenth century, came across the record book of a home for unwed mothers. There was a good deal of information in the book about the young women, their ages, what happened to their babies, and where the mothers went from the home. On a second visit to consult this account, my friend was told that the book had been "lost." In that way, the keeper of the archive was able to censor what was studied and, consequently, what was known about the local past. Moreover, the "lost" document protected the community from the shame the archivist thought the information would place on her town.

Local historians censor local history by limiting the topics investigated. There are some standard subjects that local history deals with, and there are other topics that are usually neglected: such as the study of local crime, race relations and racial conflict, the actions of strikers and bosses, the role of alcohol licensing, and political topics of all sorts. These are legitimate subjects to pursue but are generally about divisive moments in our past; they do not promote a picture of a unified community consciousness and a harmonious past.

Another way in which local historians censor the past is by a preference for beginnings rather than an examination of the development of a community over time or dealing with the decline of a town, a company, or a population. There is a bias for the remote past, for those first to till the land, early institutions, and how the community grew from a rude place to one of industry. A 106-page history of a city not far from my home devotes the first eighty pages to the period before the Civil War, relegating the 150 years since that time to a mere twenty pages. This surely represents a time warp in the way we perceive local history. It probably also reflects the fact that historical societies have not adequately collected the materials of the recent past. This cheats us of an opportunity to understand how the present came about and disguises the fact that we, ourselves, are living in historical times.

Historians also frequently ignore the history of technology. Yet the history of the sewing machine is important and interesting, for it eased the job of creating clothing, and we can find fascinating aspects of how sewing machines were shared within a community. The history of the automobile allows us to see how

residential patterns expanded; and looking at computer use today furthers our understanding of changes on Main Street and
in our expectations of what a local library should and needs to
provide.[2]

Local historians, for a variety of reasons, have encountered
censorship and have participated in it. We cannot always expand
on the limitations that documents present us with, but we can
examine our understanding of why we do local history in the
first place. By censoring our subjects, we shortchange our communities and ourselves. In presenting local history as always
positive, we deny the fact that the past was as controversial and
complicated as we know the present to be.

Notes

1. Martin Harwit, *Exhibit Denied: Lobbying the History of Enola Gay*
(New York: Copernicus Press, 1996). See also Edward T. Linenthal and
Tom Engelbardt, *History Wars: The* Enola Gay *and Other Battles for the
American Past* (New York: Metropolitan Books, 1996).

2. See Sharon Babaian, "Technology," in *Encyclopedia of Local History*,
ed. Carol Kammen and Norma Prendergast (Walnut Creek, Calif.: Alta-
Mira Press, 2000), 430–35. Included is a list of some significant technological advances with dates, so the community historian can hunt in local records to begin to recover these "events," which were not really
events at all—in that they did not happen on a particular date. Rather,
they were developments over time with multiple effects in our home
places. There is also a growing bibliography of the history of technology, and on specific advances, in Babaian's essay and elsewhere.

3

The Subjects of Local History

Parochial history . . . ought to consist of natural productions and occurrences as well as antiquities. . . . if stationary men would pay some attention to the districts on which they reside, they would publish their thoughts respecting the objects that surround them, from such materials might be drawn the most complete county histories, which are still wanting in several parts of this kingdom.

—Gilbert White, *The Natural History of Selborne*[1]

From the very start, local history in this country was usually about early settlers; the history of major institutions such as the first churches and schools; industries—especially those that produced a collectable product; fire companies; and railroads. These interests continued to be considered appropriate topics for local history, even as time went by. They followed closely the topics of early-seventeenth-century local history in England—the history of royal and highborn families, church parishes and clergy, and landownership and land division. These might be thought of as the established subjects of local history—the topics that made up the menu of what local historians traditionally researched and wrote about. There is nothing wrong with any of these individual subjects. The problem is that the scope of local history came to be restricted to these topics, even while there was so much more to consider. To be fair, the doing of history—both on the local level and when it became of some interest to the academy—has changed greatly over the past twenty-five years, as history in general has expanded to include previously neglected peoples and topics and as it has begun to explore new forms of exhibit.

Even with the greater scope of late-twentieth-century history there are still many more topics that deserve our consideration. This leads us to ask, why the earlier restriction? To answer we must recall who was involved with local history and why. In many cases, local history was the preserve of the well established and well heeled: people with some stake in the community who led it in those days of deference, who constituted its first families, and who established the community's first traditions. These early ways of thinking about local history hung on even in the face of social and demographic change, so that local history became the preserve of those of old stock, and the history collected and presented reflected that segment of the population. Others—African Americans, people of ethnic origins different from those who were first in a place, those who did not do well, or people who departed from a community—were, for the most part, left out of our local histories and probably would not have expected to be included in the first place. They were generally too busy getting by, trying to succeed, or moving on to worry much about whose letters were being collected in the historical society or whose history was being told.

But history has come out of that closet, and today our local history belongs to all of us, immigrant and long established, those with ancestors buried in the local cemetery and the newly arrived. But even with new inclusions, there are topics that are still generally avoided by local historical societies. And that in itself tells us something interesting.

Few local historical societies or local historians dwell on divisiveness. This might be pleasing, but it does give the impression that people in the past lived more serene lives than we do. Local history is generally considered by most people to be a way of building community; a way to "boom" the town, to promote its history, and to bring people together into a common past; or a way to understand place. That does explain why the history of local politics is rarely a topic of local history, for politics, by its very nature, is competitive. Yet what is more vital and important to a community than its politics?

What about those people who leave a town? They are most often forgotten, unless, of course, they name their next hometown for the place from which they just departed or return with wealth or interesting experiences to share. Otherwise, out-migration is rarely looked at in a critical way. Yet those who leave do so because of some siren call from elsewhere or because of a push from their starting place: a lack of jobs for young men or a lack of land might be considered sufficient reasons to feel pushed from one's home place. The pull of land elsewhere has always been potent, as has the possibility of work. Local historians study the institutions of a community: the churches, schools, and industries. We are happy to focus on that which has prospered, what a place is known for, how a town or village grew, what spurred it on. It is easy to forget about the industries or ideas that failed, the lives disrupted, casting community members out of work and also depressing the local economy and outlook.

Because local history is perceived to be vital to community building, topics that are disruptive are often ignored. Few local historians consider strikes or economic downturns, those who lease rather than own land, or those who make their living, legally or not, by selling alcohol. We are unlikely to find much in written local history about lawlessness, unless it is picturesque and produced a criminal-hero. In my community we have Edward Rulloff, who murdered his wife and child and probably several others. He is recalled as a great scoundrel rather than as a cold-blooded killer, and today there is even a local restaurant named for him, though few people recall who Edward Rulloff really was.

Nor have local historians adequately explored the influence of changing technology on our communities: What happened when street lighting became possible? Where were the lights put? Who was on the electrical circuit? Who was served by the water treatment plant? Where did rubbish go, and how, over time, has the collection of trash changed? What happened as the result of airport placement? What were the debates about the route of a new road or turnpike? What happens when newspapers fade or fail? These topics are infrequently explored. Perhaps now that we are settling as comfortably as possible into the twenty-first century, topics such as these from the twentieth will take on new appeal.

I think it is important for local historical societies and local historians to delve into some of the questions raised by the twentieth century. There are a great many topics that might be considered, although there is a perceptual problem in that so much of twentieth-century history looks as if, or is regarded as if, it is national rather than local history. It can, however, be both. Following are some suggestions for twentieth-century topics:

- If World War II is a national question, the issue of who became the officers of the local selection board and how that board functioned is a local topic.

- If the passage of the Nineteenth Amendment is a national question, how local men and women reacted to the long fight for suffrage is certainly a local topic. Who was for suffrage, and what were the common traits that bound them? Who was against it, and how did they express their displeasure? Was the local fight fought on the same grounds as the national battle? Was leadership local, or did it come from outside the community? What was the effect on the politics of the place with new voters on the voter roles after 1920?

- If the abortion debate currently going on is a national issue, it is also local.

- Race is probably the most difficult topic we have to deal with in this country. How have questions of race played out locally? Were African Americans mentioned in the nineteenth-century newspaper? Were there racist cartoons? What housing patterns pertained? What were the places the races mingled? In the twentieth century did the Depression touch blacks and whites in the same way, and were both aided by state and federal programs? What were the issues the races battled over or didn't discuss at all, and what were the issues that brought them together?

- Consumerism has created a new society: What about it can be documented locally? What new products are available? What are the items in demand? Is there a local style? Have easily obtainable products or stores changed the look of our communities? What about the local mall?

- Culinary changes tell us a good deal about a community over time. Can we define the local ways in which a place participates in culinary trends or sets its own?

In an essay by Paul Leuilliot entitled "The Defense and Illustration of Local History," reprinted in *The Pursuit of Local History,* this French historian sets out several principles that he believes suggest the underlying nature of local history. These present interesting avenues of pursuit.[2] The first principle is that local economic history in the nineteenth century leads into the present and illuminates our present-day preoccupations. Marc Bloch, he recalls, suggested that local history, by definition, is rooted in a specific bit of territory but can move from the present back to the past and that it is important to trace agrarian history, population changes, financial history, and the history of technology. The second principle is that local history is better suited for qualitative studies than quantitative ones. He believes this because accurate figures, for agriculture, for example, are hard to obtain. There are, however, a number of quantitative studies that can be conducted at the local level. I am thinking in particular about studies of voting patterns, of the disbursal of land or of its concentration, of the rise and fall in the population of an area, of family size, and of certain agricultural products, especially those that were tracked in federal and state census figures.

Leuilliot's third principle is that local history requires a "certain flexibility, for it is a loosely knit history."[3] His point is that local history usually cannot offer long runs of statistical material on any one subject. This is a bit perplexing, for in

French *départements* and parishes there are very long runs of vital statistics; in this country, though it is younger, there are also statistics we can turn to. We are able to construct interesting historical questions to be answered by using federal and state censuses to look at the ethnic diversity of the population over time. In many places we can look at voting patterns, political party affiliation, and the growth of population density and of agricultural produce too. On the other hand, Leuilliot believes that local history is the place to study structures over time. He suggests that industries, such as a vineyard—good Frenchman that he is—can reveal the ways in which that business was run in order to make a profit.

Leuilliot calls for local history to relate to daily life. The very best example of this is a lovely book by Françoise Zonabend called *Enduring Memory: Time and History in a French Village*, a detailed study of daily and seasonal life that investigates much that we take for granted and rarely bother to document at all.[4] This study is one that local historians should pay special attention to as a model of what can be done with local documents and traditions. It is also chock-full of interesting topics that easily translate from the French scene to the American experience.

Leuilliot observes that local history provides a place to look at the history of

> things that cannot be seen, such as contraceptive practices; it is the history of things that are given, that do not have to be talked about—though so much the better if they are—such as money and its less visible confrere, thrift (we have only to remember how new French five-franc pieces became scarce shortly after their recent minting) and it is the history of the durable, of things that last over the years, of age-old traditions, or folklore, if you prefer to call it that. Here local history overflows into the history of mentalities, of attitudes toward life, death, money, and innovation.[5]

Leuilliot calls for local history to be differential, by which he means that we look at the disparity between national or regional events and those same situations at home. The history of the automobile is of great interest and can be studied as a part of our national history, but we can also look at the automobile in a locality and use one aspect of this history to illuminate the other.

There is probably no subject more troublesome to American local historians than the Underground Railroad. Conceived in secrecy, conducted in silence, it left few records to tell its story—and far too many places said to be associated with it. Sources are the main problem—the lack of them and the responsible use of those that do exist. "I had a diary giving the names, dates, and circumstances of all the slaves I had helped run away," wrote John Parker, himself an escaped slave and thereafter an aide to runaways who came through Ripley, Ohio. An account of Parker's life appears in *His Promised Land*, edited by Stuart Seely Sprague. Parker explains that as a family man, a property owner, and the proprietor of a business, he had a great deal to lose if his record book were discovered. So "as a matter of safety," he wrote, "I threw this diary into the iron furnace, for fear it might fall into other hands." This caution was shared. Parker explains that after passage of the Fugitive Slave Act in 1850, "everyone engaged in the work destroyed all existing evidence of his connection with it." The work of aiding fugitives, however, continued apace. "In fact," he writes, it was "more aggressively than ever [pursued,] which speaks well for the conscience and courage" of those involved.[6]

Under the circumstances, it is easy to see that the sources for the study of the Underground Railroad are difficult to come by and why those that have survived are especially to be treasured. It is also easy to understand why local enthusiasts, eager to find evidence of abolition activity, have expanded on those sources using local folklore and historical fiction, willing to suspend critical analysis at the very time when we need to take the most care. Yet, precisely because reliable information is scarce, the local historian of the Underground Railroad needs to be even more vigilant regarding the subject. A casual collection of the oral and the supposed, the romantic and the impossible, brings doubt down around the entire topic—which is exactly the opposite of the desired result.

About no other local topic, except possibly the weather, are there more legends, more hearsay, more dubious claims, or more details to question. Yet footnotes, when they appear, tend to recite earlier works that contained no notes—sources that are dubious at best. In a field in which much information has been gathered orally, it is important that the reason be given why an informant deserves to be believed. In one article on the Underground Railroad the author cites an undocumented and untrustworthy church history, a pamphlet written without footnotes, and repeats stories heard from a variety of people, not all of whom are credible. There was, however, no way to differentiate among them.

Throughout upstate New York there is no topic more hotly debated than that of tunnels. There was once a tunnel, "they say," from a local temperance tavern to the lakeshore, a distance of at least a mile, through which escaped slaves were supposed to move on their way to a boat ride further north. The terrain in this part of the state, where this legend was collected, is glacial deposit—sometimes ten inches or less of soil resting upon shale. The critical mind notes that today when the New York State Department of Transportation improves a local road it brings in an assortment of yellow work trucks that include dozers and bucket loaders and jackhammers, and sometimes it even resorts to the use of dynamite to blast through the rock. If that is what happens today in order to dig out side ditches and improve the roadbed or to create a new road altogether, then it seems logical to conclude that in the 1850s a farmer with nothing but a shovel and ax is unlikely to have dug a mile-and-a-half-long tunnel for escaping slaves. The time and labor alone should cause us to doubt. Nonetheless, tunnel myths abound! A disbelief in tunneling does not diminish the fact that there was Underground Railroad activity in the area. To separate fact from fiction is the historian's job, and it can be done knowing full well that genuine accounts present us thrilling stories needing no embellishment.

There are good sources, of course, in addition to Parker's diary or the notes published by William Still and others. From

Troy, New York, there are particularly helpful and illuminating references in a local newspaper in which the Vigilant Committee reported that fifty-seven persons had passed through their care in the previous year at a cost to the society of $125.40.

In Ithaca there was a lawyer named Ben Johnson. A local historian reporting on Johnson's efforts to aid escaping slaves wrote that Johnson would claim he was a Christian, and a lawyer, and a Democrat, and therefore a law-abiding citizen, meaning that, as such, he could not assist in depriving men of their property. But, as the local historian explains, Johnson's words of self-definition would be accompanied by him handing over $5.00 or $10.00, directing the agent to "take it and buy tickets, and send the runaway slaves back to their masters." He knew, and others knew, that the money for tickets would be used to send runaways further on their way "toward the North Star." Thus, saying one thing and meaning another was Johnson's way of abiding by the law and breaking it at the same time.[7]

That there was abolition activity on behalf of fugitives is something on which we can all agree. The extent of the aid is another thing altogether, and it demands that we be cautious. We know that some fugitives came through the area. But we do not know much about the extent to which they were feared, resented, or even reported to the authorities. Especially important to remember is that those who aided fugitives frequently did so in a climate of local hostility.

John Parker noted that in Ripley, Ohio, there was considerable Underground Railroad activity, yet "the town itself was proslavery as well as the country around it." Antagonism, in the form of attacks against those involved in underground activity or in a lack of willingness to aid or to participate, is very much a part of the story to be told.

An important question to ask is, why should so much interest in Underground Railroad history erupt at the end of the twentieth century? There are many possible answers. By century's end the generation that fought World War II had aged, and those people began to tell their own stories. The book *Lest Innocent Blood Be Shed: The Story of the Village of LeCambon and*

How Goodness Happened, the book and movie *Schindler's List* (1993), and other works, fictive and real, have created great interest in and sympathy for those who risked their lives to aid the Jews of Europe a half century ago. The Underground Railroad provides an American counterpart to that activity and to the moral choices posed a century earlier. The Sanctuary Movement of the 1980s, in which some Americans gave aid and shelter to Central Americans who fled to this country, might also have spurred interest in the historical activity.[8]

Recent popular fiction has addressed the topic too. There is David Bradley's complex novel, *The Chaneysville Incident,* and Miriam Grace Monfredo's *North Star Conspiracy,* in which her Seneca Falls librarian-detective Glynis Tryon solves a mystery that originated with escaping fugitives from the South. The Underground Railroad has long been a subject of interest to novelists. *Fire Bell in the Night* by Constance Robertson is one of the earliest books of this genre.[9]

In addition, Underground Railroad activities have been featured on television shows, and the topic is an active destination on the Internet. There was a well-publicized walk along a supposed route and postings online about this journey. In Buffalo there is an Underground Railroad tour one can take, and, of course, there is a new museum devoted to the experience of those escaping slavery being created in Cincinnati, Ohio. Newspapers, too, have cited Underground Railroad sites as tourist attractions, communities have publicized them on historic markers, and historical sites eagerly make connections to this activity. Most importantly, local historians have turned to the subject in their search for understanding and illumination of African American local history, which until recently had been long neglected and is still difficult to research.

These are symptoms of current interest in the subject. The most overriding reason for a revival of interest in the history of Underground Railroad activity is surely that in this nation, where race has been identified as among our most pressing national concerns, tales of the Underground Railroad soothe misgivings about the nature of that conflict. They stress interracial cooperation, giving some people a way of asserting moral correctness about the position they think they would have taken—or that their communities did take. This is because actions of those involved in the Underground Railroad rested on what we see as clear moral choices; it is easy for us to reduce the whole issue to right and wrong. In truth, it was much more complicated. Underground Railroad activity becomes a symbol of positive behavior in our long national anguish over race. Abolition and Underground Railroad activity help us prove to ourselves that all white people were not guilty of racism, that blacks, whites, and Native Americans did take actions we can look on as moral when they gave succor to the fugitive escaping an unjust situation. These earlier positions echo through the ages the message that racial cooperation is possible.

But desiring to claim the moral high road and finding evidence to do so are two very different things. And while the public is often willing to suspend critical thinking regarding the Underground Railroad, and while local publicists and local color writers tout cultural tourism and actively incorporate every shred of evidence or hearsay into the local story, it is clearly incumbent upon the local historian to proceed with caution.

And this is exactly what I have found local historians are doing. In the face of a general disregard of the facts on the part of teachers, journalists, and others, joined with a desire to find links that make a community, or group, or individual look good on this topic, it is the local historians who are saying, "Wait! Let's look at this to see what the facts really tell us, what we can honestly assert." The problem, however, is that schoolteachers in particular and others in general are so eager for any information that they hastily incorporate whatever is available without distinguishing between that which might be credible and that which is not.

This does not mean that we should abandon interest or research into the story of the Underground Railroad. It does mean that fact needs to be separated from folklore—not every root cellar was a hidey-hole or evidence of abolitionist activity and not every Quaker household aided fugitives, although many did—that we must judge the evidence carefully and put the story of the Underground Railroad into its community context. This means we must admit that locally there were many people—often the majority of the population, as Parker suggests—who were unwilling to aid fugitives and even anxious to turn them, and those helping them, over to the authorities.

The story of the Underground Railroad is more complicated and more interesting than simply one of escaped slaves and those who aided their progress north. The story is really the story of community conflict, of moral decision making, of the law-abiding—who did not aid fugitives, even if they might have wanted to—and of those courageous people who took risks in order to lend a needed hand. The story is also of communities known as safe and those that were decidedly unsafe. It is the story of a shifting network of routes that changed with time and local attitudes, one particular route used on one day, a different way used on another. It is the story of churches that split apart over this issue and of ministers finding ways to justify the return of slaves because they were under the aegis of the laws of Caesar, not the laws of God.

All of this makes the Underground Railroad even more interesting and important because in context it becomes evidence of courage and moral character. It is and will remain a story of helpers who willingly risked their own safety to aid those in need, and most importantly, it is the story of the slaves themselves—some well known like Frederick Douglass or Harriet Tubman, but most not—who dared to escape.

We need to relate what is verifiable within a local context. We need to stress the ad hoc, unsystematic nature of the passage of fugitives from the South. We need to acknowledge the risky nature of giving aid and the unwillingness of good people to do so. And we need to celebrate the genuine heroes of the era. John P. Parker of Ripley, Ohio, was certainly one of them. But so, too, are the local historians today who are being careful with the work that they do concerning this subject and are true to what they can document.

If the history of abolition is difficult because of a lack of documents, there are other previously neglected subjects for which there is a great deal of material: architectural history, changes in the environment, agricultural innovation, educational history, the history of local communities as they change to serve the greater public demands. These topics all come with ample documentation, as does even the history of what we eat.

In newspapers, tucked into books, jotted in journals, and written in diaries or at the back of account books, Americans, especially women, recorded recipes. I have read the directions for making worm tea to cure the ailing, mixtures to take out stains, and cake recipes like this one for Jell Cake, dated 1869:

> 2 cups sugar
> 3/4 cup butter
> 2 cups flour
> 3 eggs
> 2 tsps. cream of tartar
> 1 nutmeg
> 2 teaspoon of soda dissolved in a cup of sweet milk[10]

Our recipes today come with a few more directions, but we, too, pass them along on small cards, include them in letters, tear them from newspapers, and even file them on our computers.

The historical material includes directions for making cakes and pies, jams and jellies, cookies and vegetable dishes; suggestions for tonics and "physicks"; and any number of cleaning solutions sure to remove dirt and stains. And there is no better place to look for information about the household than in our home communities. Household and culinary information tells us about ourselves as individuals, as members of families, of ethnic groups, and of geographic communities with specific traditions. Culinary taboos and preferences play out in the locality: the appearance of vegetarian restaurants and a boycott of certain foods on the basis of politics or morality are significant local events. Culinary history is also an excellent place to observe the advance of technology. Recipes preserve past foodways, while they also provide information about the production of local foodstuffs and their uses. They reflect the introduction of new foods and illuminate cooking techniques now long abandoned. They also tell much about the

technology of the kitchen—technology that has consistently trans-
formed work in the home and linked home to market.

When I think of my recipes, they fall neatly into two categories: those before I acquired a Cuisinart and those after 1977.
My food processor allows me to make a variety of dishes I had
not cooked before or had cooked once and decided they were too
time-consuming or bothersome to prepare again. This same
"revolution" occurred for women who gave up the open hearth
for a cookstove and for those who moved from cooking with
wood to gas or electric stoves and ovens. The microwave has
further revolutionized kitchen capabilities while creating new
habits and possibilities. Consider this new means of food preparation and the foods that have been created specifically for it.
Consider, too, the microwave in terms of what it has meant for
women who work outside the home.

Old recipes help us date the appearance and acceptance of
new foods. We know, for instance, that a recipe was devised after
1900 if it calls for iceberg lettuce because it was after that date that
iceberg was developed to fill the need for a lettuce that would ship
well while remaining fresh and attractive. Not only do recipes reflect information about ingredients and techniques, about families
and individuals, they also testify to regional specialties—about
things that draw people together in patterns of identification with
place. I think immediately of Buffalo wings, New England chow-
der, beignets of New Orleans, blue corn piki bread at the Hopi's
Second Mesa, Wallapa Bay oysters, South Carolina hickory-
smoked pork, ambrosia (that green Jell-O studded with marsh-
mallows found everywhere in Iowa), *spiedes* of Binghamton, New
York, and *fasnachts* in Ephrata, Pennsylvania. These, and many
others, are foods that depend on and celebrate local produce.
Though eaten elsewhere, they are linked specifically to place, and
they enhance the definition of place.

The sources for this rich culinary history exist in our archives,
like preserves on a shelf, awaiting our interest. They tantalize but
also puzzle us. Some are difficult to understand because the terms
used mean little to us today: the ingredients are unfamiliar, the
techniques unusual. Some of the recipes are difficult for us because we are accustomed to precision of measurement, whereas

many of those older recipes call for a pinch of cloves or a handful of flour.

Most of us would have little interest in actually cooking and serving many of those old recipes because they reflect a different era or dated thinking about what is healthy or fashionable. An article a few years ago in the *New York Times* published just before Thanksgiving noted, "An amble through the old recipe file is a walk down a most unhealthy memory lane. There's Mother's turkey stuffing, rich enough to clog several arteries; her sugar rich cranberry mold in its base of Jell-O; the casserole featuring Velveeta cheese." My aunt's collection of family recipes directs me to use one dozen eggs in her sand cake and nothing but butter, and lots of it, in Christmas cookies. She also calls for rose water and glycerin. The last two ingredients I can purchase from my druggist, though I am unlikely to do so, the butter I forgo, and there is no way these days that I would put one dozen eggs into anything.

While we might not want to serve these dishes today, those recipes of fifteen, or fifty, or one hundred fifty years ago tell us about food preferences of another time, about food fads, culinary influences, and health considerations. They reveal the culture of our cuisine. Times change, health concerns change, and our culinary habits follow.

Our historical interest in food mirrors our contemporary obsession with food. Look at the shelves of any bookstore and count the number of new cookbooks. Look at the magazines devoted to cooking. Think, too, about the current popularity of the personal memoir, in which food and food habits often reflect the stability (and idiosyncrasies) of family life.

There is a growing academic interest in food and food history. *Food and Foodways* is an international journal devoted to the history and culture of food. *Food History News* also relates culinary history, mostly that of North America. And on the Internet there are thousands of links that appear when one requests items about food and history.

Sandra Oliver, who edits *Food History News* from her home in Maine, is also the author of a book that is a perfect blend—or roux (a mix of flour, butter, and heat), if you will—of food, history, and place. The book, published by the Mystic Seaport Museum, is called *Saltwater Foodways*.[11] Oliver, who practiced open-hearth cooking for some years, has studied the area's foodways and related them to specific physical sites open to the public at Mystic Seaport. She carefully discusses the food that would have been cooked in a seaman's cottage, foods and their preparation in the home of a merchant family, foods available, technological changes in the kitchen, and storage of food in a more affluent home. She also looks at the food served on whaling ships that put out from Connecticut harbors and at the ingredients that might have been encountered in foreign ports, the food offered and the role of a cook on fishing vessels, and the foodways of those who made their livelihood working in a local lighthouse.

Oliver touches on the etiquette of food in different settings, storage problems and solutions, different cooking techniques, the changing cast of characters who actually prepared meals, and the cultural implications of meals eaten together and those "taken on the run." This book, which looks at the foodways of people along the southern Connecticut shore, is an important beginning for an understanding of North American foodways. It can only be hoped that Oliver's broad research plan, beginning with architectural evidence and ranging widely through library and archival records, will be followed and adapted by others to develop information and discussion of the foodways of other parts of the country.

Now is the time for researchers to dig out the recipes and directions buried in letters and diaries to help define the foods that Americans ate, learn about the introduction of "foreign" ingredients and techniques, and look at the relationship of farm to market and how that expanded because of transportation technology. We should begin by defining the terms used, the foods eaten, and the various methods of preparation in order to understand our culinary history and appreciate that which has continued from one generation to another and that which has changed.

In addition—and this will hardly prove unpleasant—we should document the foodways of our own time by collecting information about those little places that prepare local specialties and the roadside stands and regional festivals that feature foods that define an area. In this, Jane and Michael Stern have pioneered. See their *Roadfood and Goodfood* for starters.[12] There are some tasty dishes to sample and much to learn when we look up and cook up the recipes in our local archives. *Bon appétit!*

For some time now, I have kept a list of topics that local historians rarely tackle. I mentioned this to Bruce Weilepp, of the Pacific County Historical Society, in Washington State, with whom I have had a long and very interesting e-mail correspondence. He added some additional topics to the discussion.

There are many reasons why particular historical subjects have been ignored. In some cases it is because the topic is not seen as important or community building, which is what many regard as the purpose of local history. In other cases the sources for a particular study are scarce or difficult to use; some subjects require skills local historians do not have or do not care to learn—mathematics, for example, or accounting, or a foreign language. In some cases, the subjects have simply not dawned on those of us who do local history—their time has not yet come—or they do not interest us personally.

In some cases, historians have tackled these topics, so I do not want to imply that they have all been totally ignored. But I find these subjects all too infrequently treated in exhibits, discussions, and even local historical society pamphlets. And I wonder why. See what you think:

- In reading nineteenth-century newspapers I have been struck by the frequency with which the excise laws are mentioned. *Excise?* Well, I looked up the word, remembering it only vaguely from a long-ago college history course. Excise is the duty levied on the manufacture, sale, or consumption of commodities within the country. It is the opposite of import duties. Excise is not something I get very excited about these days, but then, I don't own a sports team needing a license or run a company whose products are regulated, such as tobacco.

In the context of nineteenth-century local history, how-ever, excise laws meant, among other things, the taxation and regulation of alcohol: who could sell beer, liquor, and wine; when; to whom; and under what conditions. Excise laws also meant revenue from licenses sold and taxes col-lected. Who got those licenses in a locality is important to know because permits often followed political power. How saloons, inns, and hotels sold alcohol was a matter of local concern, especially after the rise of the temperance movement.

So excise laws are important. They can tell us a great deal about how a community worked, about local con-cerns and needs—for revenue and for the regulation of al-cohol—and also about local political power. All this was, of course, before the advent of Prohibition, when the story changes and becomes even more interesting.

- This leads to another neglected topic. Rarely are there local studies or exhibits about community politics. Now, I know that often there are displays of political memorabilia—campaign buttons and posters, for example. And there are also talks and discussions about significant political shifts such as in 1856, when the Republican Party made its ap-pearance, or in the 1928 presidential campaign when Al Smith ran and ruffled the prohibitionists' feathers. But long-term political studies by local historians are few. The reason for this is surely that politics is viewed as divisive; it represents a rift in the community.[13] Yet we have ne-glected an important aspect of our community life by not looking seriously at local politics. Consider the amount of space given to politics in old newspapers—in fact, in my community, as in many others, the local newspapers were organs of different political parties or viewpoints. Consider the amount of time and energy spent on local issues and then, every two or four years, on national issues reflected through a local lens. How often has local political history been researched?

- Strikes are another topic more often neglected than addressed. Of course, certain major strikes are known, such as the Homestead Strike of 1892, the Pullman Strike of 1894, and the coal strike of 1902. But rarely considered are the attempts by labor to organize and improve conditions locally, prodded into being either by local factory conditions or by outside forces. Unions represent important efforts on the part of working people to better their conditions—to raise pay, lessen hours, make the workplace safe—and have organized representation in negotiations with factory owners. Yet the history of union formation or local strikes is rarely tackled by local historical agencies, possibly because the owners of factories were more likely to support a historical organization than was labor. As we expand our idea of who is a proper research target, the people on the picket line should be part of the picture.

- Another aspect of labor history is the role of children and youth. Few local studies look at indentured servants, many of whom were children. Child labor is more often researched and written about in a national setting than on the local level. What were the working conditions for children? Who worked, and how did that work change over the course of the past two centuries? Where did child workers come from, and how was their labor used and regulated? In my community, most child labor was probably to be found on the farm, and many of the children were local orphans turned over to farm families—their labor in exchange for food, clothing, and sometimes schooling. But there were also children involved in the cigar industry and other factory work, and we have few local studies of this important issue. In addition, who accepted indentured servitude, how long did it last, and what were the conditions required when the time expired?

- Debt is another neglected subject. Certainly debt is an important facet of business life, especially in the life of farmers.

It raises the question of the role of banks in our communities. How have people addressed the need for new capital, how has debt been managed, and what have been the consequences of failure—of a farm or of a factory? Failure is a topic that enlarges, its consequences expanding outward rather like a small stone dropped in water. What happens when a bank fails? What happens when a major company relocates? These are issues to look at in the past, and they can be studied today as well. A local study of how workers coped with the loss of livelihood would be an important contribution to a community's self-knowledge: Where did those workers go for aid? To whom did they turn? Where did those workers find other work? Did they stay in the town, shifting to another factory; did they set out on their own; or did they leave so that the failure also caused a loss of local labor—and population?

- Equally neglected is the subject of crime. Most historical societies know and discuss dramatic murder cases. Few local historians or local historical agencies, however, have taken a close look at a docket book of a local judge or court to see what sorts of cases came to trial, how they were disposed of, who became embroiled with the law, and how the legal system served the community.

This is a *very* partial list of topics infrequently pursued by the local historian. There are a great many other subjects that need to be addressed. In fact, there are too many interesting and important topics for any one lifetime.

Notes

1. Gilbert White, *The Natural History of Selborne* (New York: Harper & Brothers [n.d.]; reprint of 1788 edition).

2. Paul Leuilliot, "The Defense and Illustration of Local History," in *The Pursuit of Local History,* ed. Carol Kammen (Walnut Creek, Calif.: AltaMira Press, 1996), 164–80.

3. Leuilliot, "The Defense and Illustration of Local History," 169.

4. Françoise Zonabend, *Enduring Memory: Time and History in a French Village,* trans. Anthony Forster (Manchester: Manchester University Press, 1984).

5. Leuilliot, "The Defense and Illustration of Local History," 171.

6. Stuart Seeley Sprague, ed., *His Promised Land: The Autobiography of John P. Parker, Former Slave and Conductor on the Underground Railroad* (New York: W. W. Norton, 1996).

7. This story is recounted in Thomas Burns, *Initial Ithacans Comprising Sketches and Portraits of the Forty-four Presidents of the Village of Ithaca* (Ithaca: Journal Press, 1904), 13–15.

8. See Philip P. Hallie, *Lest Innocent Blood Be Shed: The Story of the Village of LeCambon and How Goodness Happened* (New York: Harper, 1994).

9. David Bradley, *The Chaneysville Incident* (New York: Harper and Row, 1981); Miriam Grace Monfredo, *North Star Conspiracy* (New York: St. Martin's Press, 1993). Constance Robertson, *Fire Bell in the Night* (Philadelphia: Blakiston Co., 1944).

10. This recipe is from the 1869 diary of Carrie Manning, DeWitt Historical Society, Ithaca.

11. Sandra Oliver, *Saltwater Foodways: New Englanders and Their Food, at Sea and Ashore, in the Nineteenth Century* (Mystic, Conn.: Mystic Seaport Museum, 1995).

12. Jane Stern and Michael Stern, *Roadfood and Goodfood* (New York: Alfred A. Knopf, 1986).

13. Rita Smidt's *Lansing at the Crossroads: A Partisan History of the Village of Lansing, New York* (San Jose: Writers Club Press, 2001) is an interesting exception to this. Smidt was a participant when the Village of Lansing separated itself from the Town of Lansing; her book recounts that episode. Not everyone agrees with her position or her recollection of events, but the book is a valuable account of a time many people regard as "relatively painful."

Coda to Chapter 3

Journalists and Historians

All too familiar to local historians is the telephone call from a friendly journalist: a newspaper reporter, feature writer, or someone from the local television studio. "What do you know about the person being honored by the street renaming this morning?" the journalist will ask. When did the railroad come through? When was that church built? Who founded that business? Can you give me a quick history of the local Y? Or, what can you tell me about the Underground Railroad (during black history month); about local women of note (during March); about the celebration of the Fourth of July (you know when); about tragedies in the local lake/river/sea (usually in the summer); or about the earthquake of 1859, the tornado of 1936, the flood of 1972; Indian villages once located here, battles fought nearby; the first local schools; the community center and how it was used during the Depression; Thanksgiving celebrations in the past and the ways Christmas became commercialized—and when.

Some of this we know. A good deal we don't know—or we don't know well enough to be comfortable giving responses off the cuff, offhand, and without looking up the exact dates, the previous owners, the number of dead, the make of the car. We need to be sure of the information we pass along. We are people who like to be as accurate as possible.

But because we are good-hearted, because sometimes the question is really interesting to us, because we understand the broad impact of the media, because we want reporters and others "to get the story right," we hasten to our notes, our books, and our files. We rustle about like a deer settling into the leaves on a cold night, and if at all possible we get the needed information. That is what local historians do.

These examples highlight some of the differences between historians and journalists. As local historians we are dedicated to getting the facts right, understanding events in context, and looking for the complexities that answers to direct questions sometimes contain. We plod a bit and are cautious about how we make statements because we understand the power of the press—a power that we respect. In addition, we know that once something appears in print, it easily passes into local knowledge as gospel and is likely to be picked up and reused the next time the subject comes up. "Well, I saw it in the newspaper," is a comment frequently heard. We recognize the power of the printed word, so we try hard to be accountable. And to be truthful, we are glad we were asked rather than the journalist making a stab at finding the information and not getting it right, or only getting half the story, or being satisfied with someone's rendition, which might or might not be true.

Journalists, on the other hand, have other priorities. Journalists work with pressing deadlines, they serve demanding editors who want stories "now," and they are driven by space constraints that force them to be succinct—to boil the story down. They need answers, not qualifications, and adjustments, and contingencies. They need, most of all, to get the story, and they like getting it right. But beyond getting the facts right, journalists can do with getting them attributed to someone else—something historians cannot do or be satisfied with in the same way.

Take old Mr. Tompkins. If he tells a journalist what he believes happened at that old place on the corner during Prohibition, or about the time when those two fellas got stuck up that tree, or about crop disasters one particular year, his information can appear in the newspaper the following day as what Mr. Tompkins said, or observed, or even what he believed to be true. If Mr. Tompkins tells his stories to a historian, we follow a different route, one that includes consideration of context, corroboration, and likeliness.

I like journalists, and I respect what they do. Nonetheless, they and we operate differently. We plod a bit, poke here, think about it, consider what something means, look it over, check one more source. The journalist needs to hand in a story about the burning of the local Y—and by noon, thank you very much.

Oddly, and not clearly understood by others, there is a level of complexity posed by these questions we are commonly asked. Some of the more thoughtful and interesting questions are often the easiest to answer, whereas some of the more specific questions require the greatest amount of work and worry.

I have been asked when Christmas became commercialized. This is an interesting question, and I can give an answer that is general and yet helpful to a person seeking this information. In the 1890s, there was a definite increase in advertising in our local newspapers concerning Christmas. There are numerous illustrations, a great many large-type eye-catching words such as *Christmas* and *presents* or *gifts,* and even questions asking what the reader plans to give various members of the family, with suggestions for each. There are ads devoted to interesting and inexpensive gifts to be bought along State Street, and they are aimed at particular categories of people—such as fathers or children. In addition, there is a good deal of rather bad verse celebrating the coming holiday.

Before the 1890s—in my community—the holiday was barely mentioned in the papers until the day or week before the 25th, and there was little notice afterward. Church services got much more attention than the offerings of Brown's Cheap Store or Rothschild Brothers' emporium. So this is a question I can answer from my general knowledge of the history of this place, and I can, with some certainty, send the interested party to old newspapers where examples can be found.

It is often the simple-sounding questions that are more difficult, for they demand specificity of information. What is the history of the local Y? I could give a general outline, but without a file to consult or a history of the institution at hand, this question asks for details that must be verified. Others might know, but these are not the sorts of things that I carry about in my head or that I know with any certainty. Who were the people who brought the Y to the community? Where did the money come from? These require precision. What year was the building renovated, when was it relocated, and who was against the location of the new building? Of interest might be the sorts of programs offered, the number of children who were members, the year boarders ceased to be housed on the upper floors of the building, and when that small kitchen fire occurred. All these questions need precise answers, and most of us do not carry this sort of information around or even have it in a file by the telephone. If there has never been an article on the Y, or if the historian has never researched the question of the Y, then the answers to the legitimate questions above could take a considerable amount of time to gather.

We accommodate as best we can. Yet we cannot be expected to delve into intense research to answer a journalist's question. That is work that those in the media should do for themselves. Yet we know that they are up against deadlines and are only infrequently given much time to research a story. There is a dilemma here. A local historian told me recently that she was contacted just before the local election and asked about the racial composition of the city council if in this election certain candidates won. The reporter wanted to know if this would represent a unique situation. The historian's general knowledge would lead her to say yes, but she had no proof—at least not the sort of proof that historians require. To gather it would have entailed a long period of research in the records. Put on the spot to give some sort of answer, she bravely said that she could not guess and that if an opinion were wanted, then the reporter should call a local politician who had been around for some time. In this case, the historian referred the journalist to someone who would offer an answer. Had she done so herself, she fears that she might have been wrong and would, in any case, have had no proof with which to back up her "authoritative" answer.

We help when we can; we apologize when we cannot. But these situations are vexing, nonetheless, for they force us to use what we know in a way that sometimes violates how we historians believe we should function, and often these requests come with a time pressure that is unnatural to the way historians work. However I respond to journalists' questions, I usually feel somewhat dissatisfied. Being asked by them, however, reaffirms my understanding of the historical method, and usually I am glad I do what I do.

4

Researching Local History

This single circumstance of want of materials, would, in the absence of all other reasons, justify us in receiving with extreme distrust, the narratives of the earliest historians. Before the art of printing was invented few documents existed, and tradition furnishes almost the only materials for history. How much falsehood gathered in its progress, and how much truth, modifying and almost changing the aspects of the truths it transmitted; was lost on the way, could only be the subject of conjecture.

—Salma Hale, "An Address, Delivered before the New-Hampshire Historical Society, at the Annual Meeting, 11th June 1828"[1]

Everything that men and women have written, touched, or made is a clue to the past. Such a wide range of material demands of the local historian a variety of talents so that this evidence will yield up its secrets. We need to do more than simply accept the flotsam of the past: we must question it, consider it, evaluate possible reasons for its creation, and wonder why it has survived. Although this is an obvious way to approach a historical artifact, it is not one regularly used by all historians— a lack that has led to problems for even the most careful researcher. Many times, that which the past has given us controls our view of a particular era or episode. Let me try to illustrate the problem.

Many communities (and most secretaries of state's offices) have business incorporation papers for a mill, a business, or a small manufactory. The local historian, by dint of hard work, may discover a sales ledger, advertisements in a newspaper about the product, and even some of the products that have survived as collectors' items: clocks, bottles, tinware, pottery jugs, and the like. Put together, this varied information leads to the study of a local business—a worthwhile undertaking and a relatively common local history project. The incorporation papers for the company give us the date of the founding and the names of its officers; the sales ledger reveals the cost of the product and sales for a specific period; an advertisement in a newspaper may show us a picture of the product and indicate that it was marketed locally—it could even give its price and tell something about its use; and a specimen of the article gives us an opportunity to assess it for ourselves, to feel it and describe it.

In his 1926 history of my community, Henry Abt deals with a local industry in the following fashion:

> The Ithaca Glass Works, originally fostered by Ezra Cornell, was established in 1874 and reorganized in 1876. The main factory was burned in 1882 and a new one, on Third Street between Franklin Street and Railroad Avenue, was built in 1883. At the time the new plant was one of the best of its kind in the United States. There were five buildings, containing three eight-pot furnaces, an engine room, a mill for grinding the crucible material, flattening and annealing equipment, and cutting and packing departments. Railroads had sidings at the works. Nine thousand boxes of single and double thick patent white crystal sheet glass were shipped over those tracks each month.[2]

This represents the customary treatment of a local industry and is an honest reading of the extant materials. Duly footnoted, it easily passed into the canon of my town's past. There is nothing wrong with this style of history; it is typical of most of what we read. The documents have led historians in this direction, and we have followed them, willy-nilly. Thus, by simply surviving, by surfacing from a past era, the documents on which our business history has been based skew our attention to a particular way of thinking about this glass factory.

But is this all that we want to know about the Ithaca Glass Works or any other industry? I think not. I would like to know who worked for the company, where they lived, how much they were paid, what sort of compensation they received if hurt on the job, what happened to the workers when the plant burned, the ethnicity of those who worked there, the social organizations they established for themselves, and the receptiveness of management to the creation of a benevolent society or a union. At what age did workers start in the factory, and were all of the workers male? Did workers' children attend public schools or the local parochial school, and for how long? What were the working conditions in the factory, who were the owners, how much money did they take out of the company, and where and how did they live? If these workers lived near the factory, which I suspect they did, were there local stores in the neighborhood and did they accept credit? What happened in the summertime to these local groceries, for glass works did not produce new ware in the hottest part of the year and many glass workers leased houses for only eight months, leaving in the summertime to camp along the lake. What was the community's attitude about these workers? Were they well regarded? When the company was absorbed by another corporation, which was common in that era of consolidation, what happened to the owners? When the company was abandoned by the parent company in Pittsburgh, what happened to the workers? Did they find other jobs locally, or did they leave the area?

The available documents do not provide answers to all of these questions. Little has survived to our day about the workers in the factory or about working conditions, hiring practices, attempts at unionization, crises resulting from pay cuts in times of depression, or even of happy employees well paid for their labors and respected for their craftsmanship. Yet their history is still integral to the story of what happened at the local factory. Few working people wrote letters that have ended up in local historical societies: perhaps those letters were never written; perhaps they were never collected. Without a letter of protest about an unfair firing or letters of complaint from distributors or purchasers about shoddy workmanship, these everyday business episodes have not been written into our history. By ignoring the total story, by not probing for more than partial answers, we allow the surviving documents to shape the history we tell. This leads to an incomplete history. Workers made the product, merchants offered it for sale, and someone bought it. These are all aspects of the history of the company, but only infrequently are these various persons or viewpoints mentioned in business documents, and thus they are rarely part of the history we know.

I once met a woman who was writing the history of a small cheese factory. She knew who had founded the company and how it operated; she could explain the entire process necessary to produce various cheeses offered for sale; and she knew with some accuracy the area in which the cheese was distributed. However, because the documents did not mention the people who worked in the factory, she never thought about them as an obvious part of her study, and she was startled when I asked about them. They were, she muttered to me, "just local women."

"Aha," says the women's historian, or the labor historian, with great eagerness. But no, insisted this local historian, workers were not important because they only "came in part-time and there is no record of them." The documents we use can reveal to us only what they were designed to record. It is up to the local historian to form questions that will unveil a more complete picture of the past, a past that is more complex—and often more interesting—than we will ever know if we accept at face value only that which ends up on our desks or in an archive.

If we are really interested in finding out more about the glass plant or the cheese factory than what we are given, how do we go about it? After all, workers' letters are rarely found, and employers' reactions to strikes are not necessarily part of the business documents stashed away in the local historical society. Where, then, do we look? How do we find out what we want to know, rather than merely what the extant documents readily tell us?

In the first place, there are newspapers—and often their articles reflect more diverse information than other sources. For example, none of the documents about the glass works mentions labor unrest, but the following short notice appeared in a local newspaper: "A few days ago a number of blowers at the Ithaca Glass Works were dismissed to make room for new men. The discharged workmen made some threats and the police were called upon to protect the property. No hostile demonstration has as yet, however, been made."[3] Newspaper research is most rewarding, but it does take time, for few local newspapers are indexed, and the information in them is often only part of the story. The problem I find is that newspapers whet my interest about something but the supporting information is often not to be found. For example, there was never any other mention of the men from the glass factory displaced by new workers, so I do not know why this happened or where they went—if they found other jobs locally or if they left the community. I do not know if they received some aid from the factory, from the community, or from their churches. The story, unfortunately in this case, and so often in local history efforts, runs out.

Another approach is to look through city directories (in which a person's occupation is often listed along with an indication of home ownership) and seek out the manuscript census—presently available at the federal level up to 1930 except for the lost records of 1890—in order to locate workers by occupation and by place of residence. Using both sources of information is most helpful because the city directory, an annual production, will reveal sequential occupations that the decennial census cannot show. The city directory will also reveal changes of residence, something that is interesting to track when a renter shifts from place to place or when a home owner sells one house and moves to another. This information begins to reveal a broader view of the factory and its workers, and it may offer unforeseen rewards. Workers' names, ages, and marital status and the value of their real estate—information often found in the manuscript census sheets—help build a more comprehensive portrait. Church records may corroborate this census information and provide death dates as well. Wills or inventories might be located. Physical evidence can also be sought: houses built for the workers often still stand; cemetery records and family gravestones are often extant; and we can sometimes come across a communal memory of a factory and its employees. A photograph might have been taken at a company picnic, or a local newspaper might list company employees who participated in a special excursion. Taken together, all these bits of evidence help us create a fuller picture of what went on in the factory and who worked there. Look also at the consequences of a plant closing: Do workers disappear from the local records? Do some remain to find other employment? Items with dates send us scurrying back to newspaper morgues—if they exist—and the past becomes more and more complex. Most of what will be discovered will be about the factory, owners, and products, but it is important that we attempt to put the workers into the picture as best we can.

Can we also draw parallel pictures of employers and employees and find those places where they interacted, where the two groups met: picnics, strikes, at church? Our story becomes richer, and gradually the past yields its secrets. Frequently we cannot answer all the questions we pose about a subject, but one of the delights of pursuing local history is that, at this microscopic level, we can often find more than might be expected.

This is not easy research to pursue, and it does not always tell us what we want to know, but by attempting it we have a chance to create a fuller reconstruction of the past. We can follow up on the glass workers by looking at the *Ithaca City Directory* in which residents of the city are listed in alphabetical order.[4] Without knowing the names of the workers, of course, we cannot look them up, but we can scan through the occupations listed for entrants and create our own list. Once we have names, we can see which other family members are listed (as most adults were in the 1880s), and we can plot their places of residence on a local map. Here are some of the city directory entries for the As and Bs; the letter b before an address indicates that the individual boarded and was not a home owner. What is immediately interesting in this list, of course, is the number of workers who owned their own homes:

Andrews, William R.	glass factory	51 Esty Street
Andris, Gustave	glass factory	70 Willow Ave.

Arc, Gregory	glass factory	23 Auburn St.
Arc, Joseph	glass factory	23 Auburn St.
Ballsizer, Valentine	glass factory	Hancock & Third
Barker, Charles	glass factory	47 N. Fulton
Barrett, Howard	glass factory	b. 81 Cascadilla St.
Baur, Joseph	glass factory	44 W. Mill
Bean, William	glass factory	b. 34 Hancock
Bertram, Adolf	glass factory	48 Hancock
Bierbrauer, George	glass factory	b. 10 Lake Ave.
Boland, James	glass factory	b. 6 Lewis St.

(And so on down the list.)

In all, there are 119 workers listed for the two glass companies in town, plus M. H. Heagany, the superintendent of one of the factories. Divided in half, that would mean that each factory employed approximately sixty people. I do not know, however, if the companies were exactly the same size; one might have been larger than the other and, therefore, might have had a slightly larger workforce. Many of the workers have names that might indicate they were born elsewhere, but relatively few are Irish—an interesting fact, for a substantial number of Irish settled in this community during the 1840s and 1850s. One of those listed is surely a woman. She was most likely the secretary to the company president; another person might be female, although the name is no firm clue.[5]

What do we learn from this exercise? If we chart the residences of these workers, we find them clustered in two sections of the community, both adjacent to the factories. Only one man of those listed had a long, and potentially difficult, walk to work. He lived two-and-a-half miles away on South Hill, and in bad weather he would have had an uncomfortable trip to either factory. If we then take these one hundred twenty names and group them by the streets on which they lived, we can go next to the state manuscript census for 1885 or the federal census for 1900, locate those streets, and track down even more information.

From the census, we can determine the number of resident aliens working in the glass industry; we can find out how long they had been in the community; we can learn their ages, whether they owned their own homes or rented, and if they were literate; and we can learn about their dependents and if minor children were attending school. An interesting side note emerges from this material: although many of the community's laborers who are listed in the city directory had wives who worked as domestics around the town, not one glass worker listed a female—wife, mother, or daughter—who did such work. This suggests that salaries in the glass factories were adequate to support a family. The census, by listing individuals' occupations and the value of homes, can help us determine whether this general impression is true. Neither the city directory nor the census is absolutely infallible, but research in them can help us draw an interesting group picture of people so often neglected in our local history. So, too, can Sanborn Fire Insurance maps, those useful and detailed area maps, if they are available for your community.[6]

Of the 119 glass workers there are at least eight cases in which we can locate more than three members of a family sharing this same occupation. This may suggest that those individuals felt that employment at the glass factory supplied them with enough money to meet their needs and that they encouraged other family members to join them. If the pay had been poor, or if working conditions were intolerable, it is unlikely that a man would willingly bring his sons and brothers into the factory, though in many cases even disagreeable or dangerous work was welcome when other opportunities were not available.

Documentary material for any community is usually incomplete. The next diary in a sequence telling of a woman's struggle with her religious beliefs, the key letter of a series from a soldier on San Juan Hill, or a bank account book that would allow the researcher to understand a particular failure is invariably the missing link. So, too, the senior citizen who lived through a special event always seems to have died the week before a historical investigation begins. How many times have you heard: "You should have been here last month when Mrs. Evans could have told you everything. But she just died." Even if these crucial

pieces of evidence were available, would we be able to understand the past fully?

Probably not. A soldier on a battlefield can only report on the
action of his platoon or the small group of buddies near him. He
does not know about the battle down the line or in the next
woods. A minister can only give us his view of a church schism;
even if he understands the reasons why the parishioners on the
other side oppose him, he is not always the best witness to their
concerns. A father can only tell us his version of his son's decision
to seek his fortune elsewhere—and even if he can empathize with
his son's wanderlust or desire for greater gain, his understanding
is affected by his own love and desire that his child be safe and
nearby. Our evidence is skewed right from the start; we must always seek its internal bias even before we accept its testimony.
Understanding that, we can go on to ask questions of the materials we have and extend our knowledge of the past beyond the limitations of our documents. Our questions about past events, about
prior institutions, traditions, and habits, should never be limited
by what is apparently available. We must always feel dissatisfied
with the documents we use, so that we do not simply accept what
is given but, rather, seek for all that may be of interest.

There is no rule or set of rules that tells us when we have
looked far and long enough, or searched fully, or asked enough
questions to feel certain that what we say is correct or that our
search is done. Many historians would prefer to have at least two
pieces of independent evidence to be assured of any fact. Being
absolutely sure about the past, knowing that you know accurately, depends on several things. The first is thorough research,
the second is general knowledge of the area and the period, and
the third is contemporary knowledge or judgment about the
place you are describing and about human nature. But there is a
fourth ingredient in this process of knowing—and that is an
imaginative, intuitive response to the past based on knowledge
of place and time.

For example, in Ithaca in 1823, citizens banded together to
found an academy.[7] That is a fact. About the academy there is a
good deal of information. I know the people who were involved
in the venture, who contributed to it, what the newspaper

thought about it, the hopes community members held out for it, and the benefits they believed that they would reap. I have notices of the opening of classes, the cost, and the subjects to be studied. I know the names and backgrounds of many of the teachers, and I have several end-of-year catalogs in which the students, their courses of study, and their grades are listed.

I know a great deal about the community and about the traditions from which these people came. There is one thing, however, that I do not know from the facts, and that is why this small academy in this very insignificant village in central New York admitted both boys and girls. Single-sex academies were the norm throughout New England; even in central New York, in the larger towns and nascent cities along the major route west, academies were ordinarily segregated by gender. Yet in Ithaca and in some of the smaller communities south of the Great Western Road we find coeducational institutions—at a time when many learned people believed that too much education was detrimental to the development of females and that males and females should not be educated together. Why, then, in the 1820s in Ithaca, Homer, Cortland, and Moravia were the schools coeducational?

There is nothing written in the sources that answers this question, and yet I think I know the answer. I know it because of my work in the primary sources, because of general knowledge, and because of my understanding of what sort of place this small village was. I know it also because of what I think I know about people. My speculation is that in communities such as Ithaca and Homer, where there was a tiny population, there were probably too few families with enough wealth to maintain two academies—one for boys and one for girls. So only one was built, and those who wanted to educate their children sent boys and girls to the same building. In that schoolhouse, the boys had one entrance, the girls had another, and the primary classes were segregated. The upper-level courses, however—where there were but four or five students to take mathematics or Latin—were open to any student academically prepared to enroll in them.

I am fairly certain that the size of the village and the economics of one institution rather than two provide an answer to the question of why our particular academy taught both boys and girls. But I cannot footnote such an assertion, and I certainly cannot prove it. Knowing history depends on a great many things, and knowing with real certainty will not happen all that often.

In the first edition of this book I included a discussion of types of documents a local historian is likely to encounter, along with comments about the problems inherent in those documents and the possibilities they might present. My comments were drawn from my own experience as a local historian and filled with what I hoped were "wise" words. This section is somewhat harder— or easier, depending on one's outlook—to write today. It is harder and easier for the same reason, and that is that there are now other books to which I can readily send the reader that take up the discussion of sources for local history in a thorough, if not such a personal, way.

The first of these references is *Nearby History: Exploring the Past around You,* published by AltaMira Press and the American Association for State and Local History (AASLH), now available in a second edition dated 2000. This book, put together by David E. Kyvig and Myron A. Marty, sets out to address "the gulf between academic, nationally oriented history, and nonacademic, locally oriented history." The book is chock-full of references to historical guides, subjects, and methods of doing history. I find the specialized books in the series that followed *Nearby History* particularly helpful for historians interested in the history of houses, church or educational history, banks, and other aspects of community life.

The second book is the *Encyclopedia of Local History,* also published by AltaMira and AASLH in 2000, which my friend Norma Prendergast and I edited. In this book, there are essays about sources historians can expect to find and those sources that local historians should seek out, including comments on newspapers, diaries, letters, the federal census, photographs, and other documents. There are essays about ways of doing history that note the classic books in each field, essays about social, economic, western, women's, children's, family, public, and architectural history. There are also articles about local history as it is practiced around the world (New Zealand, Scotland, Germany, England, Canada, France, and more). These essays have all been written by experts. Each writer was asked to discuss his or her field of expertise, to explain what the opportunities were, to answer the questions most frequently asked about that field, and also to identify those questions that people do not necessarily know enough to ask. I recommend that you find a copy of the encyclopedia, open it to something that interests you, and then browse about in it to see what else you might find. It is loaded with wisdom, good advice, and good humor.

With these two books, local historians can look up what they need to know about the mechanics of doing local history. That makes my job here somewhat easier, and so I leave all these topics to other books to cover. In any case, both books should be part of any local history library.

My hometown had three written histories prior to the publication of my history of the county in 1985. Two of these earlier books were collections of short articles on various aspects of the past. They were compiled in the nineteenth century and are county histories of the standard type. Both of these earlier volumes contain information of great use to me, although there are no footnotes. These volumes focus on the development of the area, its leading citizens, and its civic advancement: that is, the creation of churches, the establishment of schools, and the purification of water. The third book is a town history printed in 1926, again without footnotes, although it does contain a bibliography. The thrust of this last history is the development of local institutions, such as churches, businesses, and voluntary organizations; the origins of manufacturing establishments; products made locally; good works in the community; and fraternal and church organizations. Its interests mirror those of the 1920s.[8]

In these books, and in some others in my library, I keep an "anti-index"; that is, on the inside back cover of those books I write in the topics that I sought within them but could not find. This is not a list of charges or sins of omission committed by those earlier authors. Rather, my anti-index works in a positive way to enhance my understanding of my own historical interests and the interests of my own time. When I review the topics that I have written down, I can see themes emerge, and I discover in the pattern of entries subjects that concerned me.

For example, on the back cover of the 1926 history of my town the following items not included in the book are listed:

Rulloff–Clark
crime
influx of the Irish in 1830s
American Party—Know Nothings
Ithaca Training School
Samantha Nivison
cigar workers
OAU
Copperhead sympathy during the Civil War
Inlet Mission
Italians
Greeks
Shawanebeke—Mrs. Benchley
Grace Miller White
Suffrage 1917
Immaculate Conception (Roman Catholic) Church
League of Women Voters
Roorback
Tailor's Strike

This is not a complete list, but the items give some idea of what I looked for in the book and could not find. I can group the list by categories of interest that really do reflect my, and history's, interests during the past quarter century:

- Ethnicity accounts for a number of entries, such as the Irish and other foreign-born, and the OAU—the Order of the American Union, which was a nativist organization of the 1870s and 1880s devoted to keeping Roman Catholics out of political power.[9]

- Women's history is reflected in a number of entries: Nivison wanted to establish a water-cure hospital that would train women to become doctors; Shawanebeke (or Mrs. Benchley) agitated for women's suffrage and was regarded as a local crank, though today I think of her quite fondly for her causes and ardor. Grace Miller White was a novelist remembered for her book *Tess of the Storm Country,* twice made into a movie. The Ithaca Training School was a teacher-training institute attached to the local academy; it prepared women to become public school teachers.[10]

- Deviance is another category. Under it we find Rulloff, a notorious murderer, and Guy Clark, who axed his wife to death in 1832.[11] Political deviance would account for the Copperheads, or northern Democrats, prevalent in the area during the Civil War but never mentioned by any of our local historians, yet the evidence is that there were plenty of them around "this neck of the woods."

- History of work covers a number of entries. Cigar workers were mostly women and children; men sold (and smoked) stogies, but women and children made and boxed them. The cigar workers staged at least one strike in Ithaca, as did the tailors.[12]

While the past does not change, our historical interests do. My anti-index allows me to chart the historical fashions of my own time, just as I look in older histories to see what the historical style or angle was in times past. We can look in our older histories for their time's fashions and historical questions, and thus we have yet another way of understanding those who have gone before us. We write the history of a community by asking questions that interest us today. We discover that our views of the past differ from the views of previous writers—people who were, after all, writing about the same place and with much of the same evidence available today. Yet our books are different; and so they should be, for 1896 is not 2006, and we have learned a great deal and changed greatly in terms of our interests. Simply to repeat the history of the past by reprinting it or recycling it is a great waste of human effort and resources. We deserve better than to perpetuate the bias of the past. Our attitudes today about many things are more tolerant, more accepting than those of earlier days. The history we write should reflect our own era. The future will, as it always does, find enough to complain about—we need not add to our own misadventures the outmoded attitudes and ethos of another time.

What about credit? When writing local history, what about the debts we owe to authors who have written on our topic, whether those who have informed us or those with whom we disagree? Footnotes tell the reader where we have been, what we have looked at, and why we have reached particular conclusions. Footnotes give credit to those who know more than we do about a particular subject, those from whom we have learned, and those who have advanced ideas that we have borrowed because those ideas help illuminate what we are working on. Footnotes are a map showing how we came to view the past in a particular way, they tell the reader who first said something, and they lead a reader or another researcher to additional information about a subject. Without footnotes, our work cannot be checked, and it will be less useful to others. With good or even adequate footnotes, we can take our place in the chain of human knowing—not at all a bad place to be.

Unhelpful footnotes are those that are incomplete, inaccurate, or misleading. They send readers to the wrong volume, refer to the wrong page, cite an author with incorrect initials, or lack critical information. Examples of these horrors abound. There is nothing mysterious, however, about a footnote. It is a pledge to readers and to later historians that what is written is based on evidence that can be consulted by others. A scientist publishes his or her laboratory method and results so that other researchers can replicate the experiment and go on to new investigations. For historians, footnotes serve a similar purpose.

I once worked with an elderly man on a pamphlet-sized history. When I presented the text to him, he looked at the footnotes interspersed throughout and sputtered: "No footnotes." He believed that the historian's aim was to be read, and, being a retired printer, he wanted to sell books. He feared anything that would put off the readers. "Footnotes will scare 'em away," he repeated to me at least twice weekly. The reader does not care where you got it, he believed; the reader just wants to enjoy it. "And," he bellowed at me, "I want him to enjoy it too."

I could never convince my friend to use footnotes, and our joint effort contains none. But I was wrong to give up the fight. Footnotes need not intimidate readers, who can easily bypass those little numbers and easily ignore endnotes included at the back of a book. The absence of footnotes, however, places a book in limbo. Unfootnoted books are not reliable as history because we have no way of knowing how those authors gathered their information or if the books were written from "common knowledge." (Nor are such books folklore, for they lack the methodology necessary in that discipline as well.)

Henry Charlton Beck, the author of a number of popular and unfootnoted books about legends of New Jersey, complains in *More Forgotten Towns of Southern New Jersey* about the carping way his books were received by historians. Beck's books were placed in one library where it was the policy to loan books of nonfiction freely but to charge the reader for fiction. A critic of Beck's style and lack of method borrowed one of his earliest books from the library and returned it with utmost speed. With some ostentation he placed the book before the librarian and handed over a fee. The librarian protested that there was no charge for nonfiction; but the indignant reader snorted, "My money says what it is," and out he stormed.[13] My elderly friend and Beck had similar attitudes about history. Both came into the field from the newspaper world; both were interested in telling a good story, in attracting and keeping readers; and both were rather successful at doing just that. They gathered their information where they could and from whoever had a tale to tell. They repeated what they heard in such a way as to amuse and entertain. Neither man was concerned about the study of history or about the need for one generation of historians to be accountable to the next.

But we are. What we write about our communities will be looked at in the future by people who want to write about America's hometowns, and the problem with unfootnoted history is that it presents a dead end to those who want to know how we know. If we offer no indication to future historians as to how or where information was gathered, and if there is no way for readers to check on a statement that interests them, then our work will not stand the test of time.

What should a footnote say? We local historians are not writing academic dissertations, and our footnotes need not be greater than the whole. They should be simple and to the point. A good footnote tells the reader who first said a thing, on what piece of evidence or several pieces of information an opinion has been based, and what gives a writer the authority to move an argument forward from one point to another. A good footnote contains specific information showing how a statement can be made and where evidence can be found. It should tell in what letter, located in which collection, and in what archive we will find a quotation. It should state in which book, with what title, published when and where, and on what page we can discover a similar or dissimilar argument. A footnote should allow us to unpeel a work of local history to see how the layers were built up, thereby creating the whole.

Footnotes for works of local history can be written in many styles, but simplicity might be the best rule. When quoting a letter written by Calista Hall, a historian simply states the following:

Calista Hall to Pliny Hall, 16 August 1849, in the Smelzer Collection, Department of Manuscripts and University Archives, Cornell University.

When crediting something from a diary, the notation should read:

Belle Cowdry Diary, 6 February 1857, 28, DeWitt Historical Society of Tompkins County, Ithaca.

These citations show that the material quoted, or the source that gives a reason to assert something, can be found in these places. Readers interested in seeing the quotation in its original context or reviewing its collateral information can write or visit these repositories and judge for themselves how the original information bolsters that which was footnoted.

The use of a footnote requires some judgment. Where there are several references to be footnoted in one paragraph, they may be clustered together into one note, the number appearing at the end of the block of material in the text. They should be listed in the order of their appearance in the paragraph. All other footnotes follow these basic forms:

> Calista Hall to Pliny Hall, 16 August 1849, in Carl N. Degler, *At Odds: Women and the Family in America from the Revolution to the Present* (New York: Oxford University Press, 1980), 211.
>
> and
>
> Carol Kammen, ed., "The Letters of Calista Hall," *New York History* 43 (April 1982): 209–34.

In each case, the footnote tells us where the quotation or the information can be found.

Other footnotes expand on these basic formulas by adding the number of the volume when quoting something that has appeared in a series (a serial is a magazine or periodical, something that is issued sequentially or in a series) or adding other useful information that will help the reader locate the source. If Calista Hall's letters were still in private hands, as is much of the material that local historians use, the footnote might state: "Calista Hall to Pliny Hall, 16 August 1849, letter in private collection of Mrs. Nellie Smelzer of Lansing, N.Y." The reader is told to the best of our ability where we found the information used. If we consulted church records, we might note where in the church the records were kept: "Minutes of the Ladies Aid Society, Federated Church, Brooktondale, N.Y. (records kept in the bottom drawer of the historical file in the pastor's study)." While the physical location of privately held records might change, it is helpful to note where they were at the time of use, as sometimes that will give later users a way of tracking them. Records in private hands require us to be as specific as possible about their location at the time the materials were consulted.

There is one particular footnoting problem that most local historians face, and this concerns statements found in our town and county histories. Those books are rarely footnoted themselves, and yet they contain a great deal of material on which local historians depend. To footnote directly to a county history, however, is to lead the reader nowhere in particular, for the writers (or compilers, as many were called) of county histories do not tell us how they knew what they wrote down. To question their source of information is not to question their veracity; but footnoting directly to one of those tomes is not good enough.

My personal rule is to use material in a county history only when I have other source material that corroborates that information. For example, in the "Four County History," formally entitled *History of Tioga, Chemung, Tompkins, Schuyler Counties, New York*, published in 1879, there is mention of slaves having been held in Tompkins County prior to the end of slavery in New York State in 1827.[14] In an article, I would never simply cite the "Four County History" as my source of knowledge about slavery, but I would note that evidence of slavery can be found in census compilations, in which Tompkins County is credited with having ten slaves in 1820. So my footnote would include a citation to the published census figures, reading something like this:

"Census of the County of Tompkins," *Ithaca Republican Chronicle*, 21 February 1821: 3; "Village of Ithaca," *American Journal* (Ithaca), 24 September 1823: 3; "Census of Ithaca," *The Ithaca Journal*, 5 January 1825: 3; and *Census for the State of New York* (Albany, 1855), ix.

It may be noted that with primary material leading the reader directly to the source, the inclusion of the county history, in which the mention of slavery is vague at best, is unnecessary.

What of a statement in an unfootnoted town or county history that cannot be verified? If the information is something that I want or need to use, I would then state in the text or in the footnote where the information came from and that I have been unable to verify it elsewhere, but that even while I cannot confirm it, I have no reason to doubt it. Then I use the material as I would any other, and I do not worry about it. Sometimes we have to use our common sense and then move on.

What should be footnoted? There is no firm rule that covers every case, but there are many situations that require us to give credit. When someone is quoted directly, a footnote is needed. When an author is quoted indirectly or his or her material is drawn on, credit is needed. When a fact is mentioned that is otherwise unknown or beyond common knowledge, a footnote to the source is needed. For example, it is generally known that once there were slaves within my county, and this fact need not demand a citation. When I categorically state that there were ten slaves, however, it is incumbent on me to tell the reader why I used the number ten rather than twelve or eight. My sources directed me to state ten, and I did so with conviction. I therefore credit my sources.

- A footnote is needed any time an argument is developed that coincides with an argument or disagrees with a contention of another author who has written on a particular subject.

- We need a footnote when something written is a revision of previously held ideas.

- Any time an author advances knowledge beyond that which was previously known, a footnote is needed.

- When we deviate from that which has been previously stated, we should explain to our readers what evidence induces us to think otherwise.

- If material used is gathered from an individual in an oral interview, that person should be noted or credited in a footnote. An interview with an old-time resident of the area about a flood, or education, or family history might yield useful information. An appropriate footnote will tell who gave you the information used, when you were told, and something about the authority of that individual.

My footnote for a 1935 flood could take one of these forms:

Conversation, 16 April 2002, with Sally Smith, who was forced from her home by the 1935 flood.

or

Interview with Paul Smith, 1935 flood survivor, 16 April 2002.

or

Casual conversation with Paul Smith regarding the 1935 flood, 16 April 2002.

This last form indicates that the information gained from Smith was not the result of a planned interview but, rather, was more informal in nature—in this case, I talked with Smith while I was standing in line at the grocery store.

Footnotes are important, and they are relatively simple to write. They document things other people have said, borrowed ideas, and items that have caused you to think differently. Footnotes should lead to sources, and they also show the transmission of an idea. They lead, sometimes, to more information on a subject. They do not need to scare a reader or a writer.

"But what," a woman asked me some time ago, "do we do when we cannot footnote our material?" She added that in some instances footnotes would be expensive to add to a text and in other instances they would be inappropriate. Footnotes often add to the cost of printing if they are placed at the bottom of the page, but as endnotes following a chapter or at the end of a book they add little to the overall cost: "When are they inappropriate?" I asked. The woman replied: "In a church bulletin that might carry a historical announcement, in a program, perhaps, or souvenir pieces issued by a community. What then should be done?"

It seems to me that there are two solutions to this problem. The first is to take one copy of the text, whatever it might be, annotate it with references, and place this special copy in the nearest archive. This annotation can be done on the page itself or on an accompanying sheet of paper; or if extra pages are sewn in the book, then the footnotes can be written on the interleaved sheets.

The second solution is what I call the "sneaky" footnote. This is a way of footnoting material that usually does not receive such careful treatment. A writer of local history in the public press is someone who is faced with the problem of giving credit in a medium in which editors and others would frown on and most likely delete the insertion of a real footnote. The sneaky footnote is better than nothing. Information, or as much of it as possible, can be written directly into the text. It usually does little for the graceful flow of the article, but it does manage to give credit where credit is due, and it directs readers to the appropriate source.

"As Calista Hall wrote to her husband, on 16 August 1849, in a letter donated by Nellie Smelzer to the Cornell Archives" is one way to begin a statement and give credit at the same time. Another way is to introduce a fact by noting that it "appears in the section on the Town of Caroline in the 'Four County History,'" and still another is to note that historian Carl Degler quotes Calista Hall in his 1980 book *At Odds.*

In each case, there is enough information to get an interested reader to the right archive, where the index of holdings will lead to the letter in question, or to the author's name and book title. There is enough information to be helpful but not too much apparatus to put off an editor, who is likely to regard footnotes as pedantic and antithetical to his or her idea of what should appear in a newspaper.

It is particularly important that local historians be conscientious about footnotes because often the materials with which we deal are outside common repositories and, therefore, are unknown to others. Our footnotes do more than reveal our sources; through them we share knowledge of local materials with others engaged in similar or related studies. We also show the usefulness of materials in private hands that might seem to their owners to have little general historical value.

By writing accurate footnotes, by annotating special copies of publications that are not to be footnoted, and by inserting a sneaky footnote into material not generally dealt with in this way, we local historians keep faith with those on whom we leaned—and from whom we learned—and we keep faith with those who will come after, offering our footnotes as a token of openness and honesty, one generation to another. Our responsibility, I believe, is to "leave footnotes unto others as we would have footnotes left unto us." If this sounds like a hard-and-fast rule, so be it. Consider how much easier our task would be today if the historians who preceded us had followed that rule. I can think of no more important dictum for local historians to follow. It keeps us honest, and it is our link of trust with the future.

> *Leave footnotes unto others as we*
> *would have footnotes left unto us.*

All this leaves us with one final topic to consider, and that is the issue of note taking, for it is on the quality of the notes we take when researching that we write our footnotes. There are people with hard-and-fast rules about 3 × 5 cards for bibliographic citations and 5 × 8 pads for information, whereas others prefer different sizes and even different colors of paper to distinguish among various archives. With computers, people devise their own systems that identify gathered information.

In essence, what is important is that every piece of information you take down be keyed to its source so you can state in a footnote that a particular fact or stress can be found on a certain page in a particular book, or in an archival collection, or on a map located in a map collection. I try to record all this information in such a way that I have all the details I need when I go to write. Human nature being what it is, or my habits being what they are, I sometimes fail to get everything necessary for writing a complete note, which means that I then have to retrace my own path back through the library to relocate a page number or date. Doing this once or twice should be enough to alert us to the tortures of backtracking, and it should be enough to make us careful at the outset that we retrieve what we know we will need. Going back and checking twice is simply a way of life for many historians, but taking complete citation notes at the outset is a great favor to yourself.

Notes

1. "An Address, Delivered before the New-Hampshire Historical Society, at the Annual Meeting, 11th June 1828," in *Collections of the New-Hampshire Historical Society* (1832): 125 and reprinted in *Pursuit of Local History* (Walnut Creek, Calif.: AltaMira Press, 1996), 61–65.

2. Henry Abt, *Ithaca* (Ithaca: Ross W. Kellogg Publisher, 1926), 117.

3. *The Ithaca Democrat,* 27 December 1883.

4. Henry Mente, canvasser and compiler, *Ithaca General and Business Directory for 1884–85* (Ithaca: Norton and Conklin, 1885).

5. See Graham Hodges, "History of Work," in *Encyclopedia of Local History,* ed. Carol Kammen and Norma Prendergast (Walnut Creek, Calif.: AltaMira Press, 2000), 478–86.

6. See Ed Salo, "Sanborn Fire Insurance Maps," in *Encyclopedia of Local History*, 402; and see the Library of Congress, *Union Lists of Sanborn Fire Insurance Maps Held by Institutions in the United States and Canada*—microfilm copies may be purchased from the Library of Congress Photoduplication Service and from the D. A. Sanborn Fire Insurance Company, 629 Fifth Avenue, Pelham, NY 10803; 914-738-1649; www.sanborn.map.com.

7. See M. Teresa Baer, "History of Education," in *Encyclopedia of Local History*, 146–48.

8. D. H. H., *History of Tioga, Chemung, Tompkins, and Schuyler Counties, New York* (Philadelphia: Everts and Ensign, 1879); John H. Selkreg, ed., *Landmarks of Tompkins County, New York* (Syracuse: D. Mason and Co., 1894); and Abt, *Ithaca*.

9. See John Bodnar, "Ethnicity" and "Nativism," in *Encyclopedia of Local History*, 166–68, 340.

10. See Marsha Semmel, "Women's History," in *Encyclopedia of Local History*, 474–76; and Mary Beth Norton, "Women's Legal Status," in *Encyclopedia of Local History*, 477–78.

11. See Theresa Lehr, "History of Crime," in *Encyclopedia of Local History*, 127–30.

12. See Hodges, "History of Work," and Patrizia Sione and Richard Strassberg, "Labor History," in *Encyclopedia of Local History*, 272–77.

13. Henry Charlton Beck, *More Forgotten Towns of Southern New Jersey* (New Brunswick, N.J.: Quinn and Boden, 1963), 5–6.

14. D. H. H., *History of Tioga, Chemung, Tompkins, and Schuyler Counties, New York*, 458.

Coda to Chapter 4

When Being Right Is Not Good Enough

Like many of you, I am frequently asked to review how other people use local history. I am happy to read drafts—rough and otherwise—in the belief that the more eyes that see a work before it is "carved in stone," the better.

A while ago a publisher sent me a manuscript made up of short biographical sketches of famous people linked to particular places. No sources were given as the basis for the essays, and the information seemed to have been gathered from general biographical dictionaries and encyclopedias. To start with, I was not overly impressed. But I was only a reader, not a publisher putting up money to produce this book, and I am certainly not the best judge of what will sell.

On the whole, most of the information was probably correct. I did not read and fact-check each entry, as that is not what had been asked of me. But I did carefully read the biographical sketches of people about whom I have written or done some research. While few things in those pages were actually wrong, there was a great deal that was not right—that just would not do. The author had used material without giving any thought to balance, nor had information been used with any sort of judiciousness. Let me give several examples of the problem:

- The author implies that John C. Frémont opened up 25 percent of our country, a statement that is inaccurate and goes against the grain of much current thought about western expansion. I can hear Professor Patricia Limerick say, "Opened up to whom?" and "Single-handedly?" Yeah. We can probably all agree that the western part of this country was not actually closed and that it was certainly not empty. In addition, Frémont went west as the leader of a group of men who followed him through thick and thin, and often it was very thin. I think of Herr Preuss, who complained bitterly just about every step he took in his travels with Frémont. So this statement gave me pause.

• Or, again from the Frémont selection, it is implied that he personally received the Mexican surrender of California at Cahuenga on 13 January 1847. Well, yes, Captain Frémont did officiate at the surrender. The statement is not factually false—but it is inadequate and misleading, for Frémont did so despite the fact that he had no orders from his superiors to do so and, in fact, had been told not to; in addition, and this is crucial, he faced a court-martial for his actions that day and thereafter. So although Frémont did receive the Mexican surrender (a true statement), he was reprimanded for doing so, which should certainly qualify that particular fact.

• Elizabeth Cady Stanton is linked to the National Women's Hall of Fame, a museum the author describes in detail. And, indeed, Stanton is honored there. But the facts that her house in Seneca Falls is open to the public, that the Women's Rights National Historic Park is just down the street from the Hall of Fame, and that the Seneca County Historical Society as well as the Library of Congress hold important artifacts marking the actions of Stanton and others involved with the 1848 Women's Rights Convention are totally ignored. So, yes, it is true that she is honored in the National Women's Hall of Fame, but that is only a single place in Seneca Falls where she is remembered. The statement is true but incomplete.

At the same time I was reading this manuscript I encountered an essay in *The New Yorker* by Daniel Kevles, a historian of science at Yale University. Kevles writes: "He seemed not to know that errors vary in their scientific significance, that evaluating their meaning involves critical judgment, and that discrimination in the use of data is a feature of scientific inquiry."[1] Much the same could be said of historical inquiry; research is not a matter of copying out information from secondary sources—even if that information is in itself correct. And those people who skim off the "interesting parts" of history should certainly not give the public half-truths, or partial truths, or facts that do not tell the truth. The work of the historian involves evaluation, organization, critical judgment, knowledge of context, discrimination, and thoughtfulness.

The second episode that made me think about half-truth occurred when I received a list of citations for new historical markers that had been approved by a nearby town and sent off to a foundry—which is as close to "carved in stone" as one can get. I was asked if there were any significant events that had been missed because there was money for additional markers.

As any of you who have created the text for a historical marker know, whatever the subject, writing in limited space is extremely difficult. In the text I reviewed, compression had created some odd grammatical problems and some offensive abbreviations that I was sure people in the area would not appreciate. There was also a problem with the selection of particular words, some of which were simply incorrect, others of which were historically misused, and still others of which were misleading.

There were, moreover, two general problems. The first was similar to that encountered in the book project. Compression had created partial truths by imparting a fragment of the story while skirting the real significance of the place being marked. In the process, things not true, and probably not even intended to be read as true, were clearly implied. Statements were not exactly wrong, but they certainly were not right either.

The second problem was even more difficult to explain and correct. I spoke with a member of the town board who did not care about interpretation, shadings of meaning, or even the choice of what was being commemorated—some of which was highly questionable—as long as there was nothing on these historical markers that could be proved to be "factually wrong." Yet, while most of what was written was not exactly wrong, much seemed unimportant, trivial, or outdated in its emphasis. In one case, an early railroad was commemorated, yet the fact that this was a horse-drawn line rather than a steam-powered engine was totally ignored. The signs also copied the patterns of those erected in the 1930s by naming first families, first supervisors, first mills, and other initial events—as if after its period of settlement, history in the area stopped. None, for instance, commemorated anything that had happened in the twentieth century. The implication here is fairly clear: only initial events are important.

Every piece of information about the past is not worthy of commemoration. We need to know all we can; but knowing, we make judgments. We must learn what is significant instead of using whatever has been found simply because it is old. Being a historian involves more than just knowing "old stuff"—or even knowing where to find facts. Being a historian and using history—especially on behalf of the public—depend on a delicate balance between the meaning of what is known and what is not known, placed in a carefully understood context.

Any historian asked to write historical markers, or to create short biographies of famous people, would begin with a question about why the material was wanted in the first place and to what use this history was being put. Historical markers are intended to help a particular town promote a sense of itself by the use of history. That is okay with me. But then the next question must be, what sense of itself?

In addition, historical markers should be easy to read; they should give a sense of what happened, communicate the significance of the site, and explain the events or people being commemorated. Certainly, short biographies are difficult to write. But difficulty is not reason enough to slant the truth or to ignore what is unattractive or quirky about people of the past. Fragments of the truth distort the meaning of what we are trying to convey. Shouldn't these projects reflect some of the diversity of the past, some of the humor of the human situation, some of the changes that created problems or opened up opportunities?

Doing history can appear to be deceptively simple. It does not require arcane language or technical training. But it does demand that the historian do more than simply locate facts and copy them from one place to another. History is about the questions we ask, the purposes to which we put information, and it is about careful investigation, balance, discretion, thoughtfulness, fairness, context, and, finally, clear communication. We must stand up for the fact that being right is not enough.

In response to an earlier form of this essay, Dwight Pitcaithley, the chief historian of the National Park Service, sent me a note he had received. It is worth reprinting, and I do so here with the permission of Constantine J. Dillon, National Park Service superintendent of Fire Island National Seashore. He wrote:

> Well, shoot, I've spent a lot of time preparing a terse, yet not-wrong text. Are you now suggesting that these should not be used?
>
> - ABRAHAM LINCOLN: President of the United States 1861–1865. No significant accomplishments after leaving office.
> - SANTA FE TRAIL: Popular route used by people to travel through the Midwest in the 1840s.
> - CORNELIUS VANDERBILT: Though among the richest people in America, he never owned his own car or watched television.
> - FRANKLIN ROOSEVELT: Man who is pictured on the dime.
> - AMERICAN INDIANS: Native people of North America whose numbers have declined sharply over the past 400 years.
> - 14TH AMENDMENT: Constitutional amendment coming after the 13th amendment but before the 15th amendment.
> - APOLLO 11: Space flight that took place in 1969.
> - TITANIC: One of the largest ocean liners ever built. Only used once.

Note

1. Daniel Kevles, "Annals of Science: The Assault on David Baltimore," *The New Yorker,* 27 May 1996: 94–109, quote on 102.

5

Giving Back

If stationary men would pay some attention to the districts in which they reside, and would publish their
thoughts respecting the objects that surround them,
from such materials might be drawn the most complete county-histories.

—Gilbert White, *The Natural History of Selborne*[1]

Finding out, figuring out, knowing about the past is only half the
job. For me, communicating what I have learned is the reason to
engage in local history research in the first place. If this makes
my local history efforts appear to be utilitarian in the eyes of
some, so be it. That is the way I am, and I believe that is the way
most people are. We learn things about place to understand, to
share, to tell others, to explain, and to answer questions that we,
and others, have. Anything else, to my mind, would be a one-
way conversation.

Knowing leads me to want to share, to contribute to our
common knowledge, to show or demonstrate or tell—to teach.
Learning also leads to our asking more questions, questions that
are only possible because we have learned and thought about
the local past in the first place. Knowledge begets questions; but
knowledge is not an end in itself.

Many people begin local history research because they have
a specific goal in mind. People research the histories of their own
houses or of buildings in their community to document their origins or styles—or to get them listed on an architectural register.

Others begin research about family members in order to construct a genealogy. Some people research the history of a town to write its history or of a church to discuss its background. Many people are interested in the growth of a local industry, spurred by a product they have begun to collect: a bottle, a clock, tools, postcards, even cars or railroad trains. What begins with an interest in an object often expands into a search for information about the company and then about the industry's role in the history of the community. Some begin with an interest in the item, then in how the industry came into being, perhaps to explain the coverlets marked with a date and the town name, or to document how the animal traps helped fund a different way of life. Some begin research with an eye to creating an exhibit, and in the process they share what they have learned with others. Some investigate the ways that the town has grown; others seek to document why a community has developed in a particular way or what a place used to be like. Some people engage in local history research in order to assess environmental concerns. The need to know propels most of us into local history research. We question, we have been asked to find out, we are curious—and we end up in the local archives.

Beginning with a goal means that we often tailor our research to that end. When I need to write an article for the newspaper, I research a topic with that in mind; when I need to give a talk, I search for materials to draw on for that purpose; when it is time to write a book or create teaching materials, I approach the archive with readers or students in mind. Thus it is that often we research with the scope of our research already defined. I do not (usually) spend fifty hours digging out material for a 600-word article, although I must admit that has happened. In such a small format, I can only use a bit of information so I try not to go too far beyond what will help me understand the subject of the article. Of course, I know and need to know more than I can ever communicate in such a brief space.

Some people speak vaguely about writing a book, as that seems to be an obvious goal. In some cases the book is actually completed, sometimes it is not. Often a book project hangs like an albatross around the neck as a constant reminder of work not yet completed. A book project, however, is not always the ideal format for communicating local history knowledge, and to simply assume that it is can work to our disadvantage.

Books, of course, are significant contributions. There are a number of popular local history book formats. The old 800-page county history is probably a thing of the past, but smaller, more concise works of local history will always be popular, as will books of historical photographs, of now-and-then photographs, of old postcards, and of articles gathered together around a particular topic. There is a constant need for good well-researched books that explain a subject thoroughly. I do not want to imply that a book is not a proper vehicle for the local historian to consider, because worthwhile books about local history appear every day. However, we also need articles—scholarly ones for history journals and popular ones such as those found in airline magazines and tourist brochures.

Yet not every topic needs to be presented as a book or article, and not every researcher will actually sit down to write, especially when there are so many other interesting formats for local history. The form our research takes will be determined by our own current need, by the nature of the documents we are searching, by our skills, and by the audience we hope to reach.

Exhibits are a different form of sharing local history research. These are usually the creation of historical society personnel working in local museums and sometimes in other local institutions, especially when an anniversary is about to occur. I would like to see historical exhibits in places other than historical societies. I think we need to have them in banks and buses, on street bulletin boards, in the county courthouse, and at street festivals and other community events. Only by going outside the historical society will we come into contact with people who have not chosen to expose themselves to local history and who are often surprised by the liveliness of it.

There are many other interesting ways to communicate what we learn, and there are many audiences out there whose interest in local history we should find ways to tap. Because people today have a limited amount of time and many exciting and interesting distractions, we need to think of an array of formats in which to display local history. We only get one or, at most, a few opportunities to try to draw people into knowing about the local past. Thus, we must do a good job. And that means knowing what we are talking about and tailoring the form of presentation to the audience and the occasion. Many topics fit well into a video presentation, a good exhibit, a radio presentation, or newspaper discussions, whereas other topics might best become pamphlets, posters, or dramatic presentations.

Probably the most ubiquitous form of local history, and the one encountered by the greatest number of people, is the history article in the local press. Some years ago I put out a call to people who wrote regularly in newspapers. "How did you start?" I asked. Many replied that they had been invited to write by an editor because they were known to have an interest and some knowledge of the subject; some were already on the newspaper staff and took on the job of presenting local history. One man reported that he had bought the newspaper and therefore could put into it what he wanted, so local history was prominently featured.

What are the attractions of writing for the press? Most writers liked the short length of newspaper articles, which run generally from 400 to 1,200 words for a weekly offering. (Special articles such as anniversary or commemorative pieces, and sometimes obituaries, which are an interesting category of local history unto themselves, are often given somewhat more space.) Some liked the fact that newspapers often publish pictures, which help explain the topic and often attract readers. For me one of the nicest benefits of writing a newspaper column is that I frequently run into my readers and we can talk. One regular reader is the young man who changes the oil in my car; another is the man who runs the stone quarry.

Writing local history for newspapers requires that the historian view the material in small bits. The writing needs to be lively and to the point, and footnotes need to be of the "sneaky" variety (see page 112). Topics usually range over the history of the area, not only in time but in subject and kind.

The problems of preparing a newspaper history column are few but important to note. They include writing on a regular schedule; the tricky question of using names and events of recent vintage that could upset some readers; pleasing editors while at the same time being true to the standards of historical inquiry; limited space, which is often inadequate to explain many topics fully; and breaking topics into weekly segments, which might not be totally satisfying. There is also the reality that even if one receives payment, it never begins to cover the costs in terms of the writer's time.

One of the joys, however, is that a weekly column can be a potent vehicle as the writer gains a degree of local authority, attracting materials that were previously unknown and questions from the public that are sometimes stimulating. A timely column can have an impact on a community. When a historic church is threatened by demolition because its congregation wants something modern, an article about the history of the building can make a difference (or exacerbate a split in the church or community). A school board fight might elicit an article about an earlier dispute that could help put the current battle in perspective. An election trick might bring forth an article about earlier election shenanigans. A column about diversity at a time of racial or religious tension can help a community see itself in new ways. We should be conscious of the power of the press and the power of the printed word—something that even we local historians can enjoy when writing for hometown newspapers.

What attracted me to writing for the newspaper was that the audience for local history is expanded far beyond those who profess an interest in local history. Even if people are not regular readers, a topic one week might pique the interest of some, whereas a different topic another week might attract others. A newspaper allows us to take local history to people other than those who belong to historical societies or attend exhibits and lectures. It offers an expanded and diverse clientele, crossing social, racial, and economic borders, and there are often interesting responses from readers. People call or write to complain, but they also suggest topics and sometimes they share interesting information that might not otherwise be known. Readers have sent me memoirs they have written for senior citizen writing classes, and they have offered up new words, or localisms, or other bits of information that I am happy to receive. Readers, too, alert me to anniversaries, to people, and to events that might not be known to me. Readers often remind me that though the local historian is looked to as the authority, the local historian does not know it all. In general, this is a very satisfactory form of doing local history, and after twenty-five years I have yet to run out of topics. There is always something old to write about.

There are other formats to consider. I am a fan of pamphlets for some of the same reasons that I like writing for the local press. Pamphlets—softcover booklets of up to eighty or so pages—allow us to deal with an event or a trend, a smaller segment of history. The format focuses the topic, which helps the researcher-writer focus the prose. There is an economy that I like to be found in pamphlets. Few in the general public these days will sit down to read a 400-page local history—they are generally regarded and used as books of reference. People today are busy and have to make choices about what they will read or what they will do.

Pamphlets are friendly little things. To my mind, they invite people to pick them up and read them. Promised within is not an endless discussion but a focused one—and usually one with pictures. I have a series of pamphlets I have picked up around the country, and I always appreciate the crispness of the presentation, the low cost, and the high quality.

Another form of publication is the four- to eight-page article printed as a separate offering. My model for these is the series of articles about St. Louis neighborhoods published by the Missouri Historical Society that discuss ethnic groups, municipal services, and other topics. These 8 ½ × 11 stapled articles appear in a comfortable format, are illustrated with crisp pictures of the city, and are printed on substantial paper. They are inexpensive to produce and cheap to acquire. The information all these little brochures contain could have and might have been published in book form. As such, it probably would have been bought by the same people who usually buy historical society materials—and possibly by tourists to St. Louis. Breaking down all this material into discrete segments and publishing them individually makes them attractive to residents and visitors alike. They can be given out by the historical society to visitors, and they can be acquired by teachers to put on classroom walls to show off the city in which their students live.

A number of people have turned to video as a format for presenting local history topics. I have seen some videos that I admire, and I have acted as a consultant in getting one or two of them put together, but I have no expertise about video production or about the costs. Local television stations today often offer classes to teach people how to make videos and then air them on local channels. I have seen some public television programs produced by local people on history topics with variable results—some are well done, others are not quite so smoothly presented. It all depends on the skills of the people involved and probably on the amount of money available to support the project. I would like to see more local historians use this means of communication, perhaps by tapping into the technical resources often available through local community colleges and other local institutions.

Theatrical productions, including plays, pageants, skits, and choral works, are also potent vehicles for presenting local history. Some years ago, a theater director asked me for the names of interesting local nineteenth-century women she might incorporate into a play. Later, after she had looked at some of the letters and books, she asked me to review her notes, which I did, and in the process I made an arrangement of the materials she had selected and wrote transitions that explained their context.

The script that developed was interesting, but it was only representative of middle-class women. It lacked dimension and breadth; it failed to portray a range of nineteenth-century women's lives. When I mentioned this to the director, she asked what documents could be used. I had to explain that there were none—or none I knew of—that illustrated the lives of Irish serving women or of African American women in our community.

"I could write some material for you," I ventured. I created the two characters in the drama that audiences particularly loved. One of the reasons why the fictional characters were especially approachable for both the audience and the actors is that the imagined stories were more completely realized than the snippets that came from letters and diaries of the "real" people. In addition to the fabricated characters—in order to tell the complicated story of one local woman who lived a great long time and vowed at the age of seventeen that she would definitely not want to grow old here—but did!—we put on the stage at the same time her younger and her older self, who was still, at an advanced age, a local resident and a local character.

These were departures from the actual fact, though sound dramatic devices. They made the play popular enough to enjoy several revivals over the past years. But the created characters raise the issue of fictionalizing the past—of mixing the real and the imagined. This can pose difficulties for writer, cast, and audience. The director Oliver Stone has been charged with altering facts in his movies, especially in *JFK* and *Nixon*, and his use of history has been much discussed. Overall, while most people have defended his right to artistic license, many have not approved of altering the well-known and -remembered recent past to create a fabricated story.[2] We are, however, in a somewhat different relationship to our material and to our community. After all, the local historian or the local historical society has a responsibility to promote a truthful account of the past and is looked on to do so. In addition, there are few checks or reviews of our presentations, unlike the multiple protests from many quarters that were raised about Oliver Stone's work.

One of the problems for those charged with or committed to telling the truth about a locality is that the local past is a fragile thing. With relative ease, selected tidbits enter into the public memory, and, right or wrong, they tend to stay there. It is far easier to add a new fact to what the public knows about its local history than it is to erase an error from the local record—especially if the piece of misinformation is an "interesting tidbit." Goodness knows, in my community there are several persistent myths. But, no, the Little Rascals did not originate in Ithaca, the Victorian house on Titus Street was not the model for the Addams Family mansion, and only a few scenes of our gorges and lake appeared in *The Perils of Pauline*. Removing the interesting but incorrect myths about place is a nightmare.

What, then, is my justification for creating fiction to explain the local past? I see it this way: in many cases there are too few records to represent a particular event and sometimes none for an individual. In the case of the play about women's lives, there were no documents that allowed us to put on the stage "in their own words" anyone other than white women. To have gone forward with the play without an array of local women would have perpetuated a past we all hope to expand on and not enshrine.

So Elizabeth Blackman in *Between the Lines* tells the audience about her husband, the minister of St. James A.M.E. Zion Church, and about her elder son's occupation as a waiter at the local hotel, and of the blindness of her younger child. Her name and family situation came from the census: her dramatic voice was imagined. Brigid Cain recalls her voyage from Ireland, the opportunities she found in the New World, visits to Ithaca by the priest stationed elsewhere, and the dearth of young Irishmen with the means to marry. In this case too, Brigid's name and status came from the census. These women were real people; their words, however, are imagined, made up perhaps, but as true to those women's historical situations as I understood them to be.

These two stories did not expand the local female population to all who might have been included, but they varied the participants in a way that made the play richer and more historically accurate. This is the same justification used for the costumed performers at outdoor museums, those workingmen and -women at the hearth, and even those in the slave auction held at Williamsburg several years ago. All of these events are drawn from the historical past and brought to life with words that cannot be quoted from the sources. After years of researching, learning, and reading, there are some things that a historian knows about a place that are not documented and cannot be verified.

The other reason to turn to fiction in the presentation of the local past has to do with audience. Drama, in particular, offers history in a different venue and sometimes to a broader audience than one finds in a museum setting or reading the local newspaper. Drama and other imaginative forms that use the local past are often useful ways of exploring difficult topics, especially those about which the public might have definite ideas that one would like to question or even dislodge. Where I live, in upstate New York, one of the most problematic topics concerns the Underground Railroad. Many people cling tenaciously to the idea of the railroad, claiming hidey-holes in their homes where there are root cellars, believing in a complete pathway north, as clear as a AAA map. Yet the sources are few, and truth hard to ascertain.[3]

To deal with this, I put Harriet Tubman onstage with a speech she never gave. Harriet says, in response to a question about the Underground Railroad:

> Ain't no cars, no tickets, no rails. Mostly it's cellar holes and barn lofts; it is wagons with double floors to hide in, clothes to disguise you, and trunks large enough to fit a man. The Underground Railroad is hiding places and courageous people. People willing to lie to save you even when they hate telling falsehoods. It is those with nerve to do right; to shelter the runaway and risk their freedom to do so. People who pass you on to whoever next is safe. . . . Whoever can be trusted at that moment. Sometime you go one way, sometimes another. It is not a railroad at all, but it is the route to freedom.[4]

This is not the common perception of the Underground Railroad, which by its very name has become in people's minds, and in some artists' renditions, a set route to be followed along which lived only people of goodwill.

A local theater company has toured two of my historical dramas written for children, this one about the Underground Railroad and another, called *The Day the Women Met*, about the 1848 women's rights convention in Seneca Falls. Each presentation was seen by over fifteen thousand schoolchildren. And each presentation was followed by a question-and-answer session during which the students had a chance to ask the actors questions about the play, about the historical background, and even about the actors themselves.

We knew that the plays worked, for when Harriet Tubman appeared from the bushes carrying her gun, every head in every single audience swung in unison to the left. When Frederick Douglass gave his speech at the 1848 convention there was absolute silence. We knew that the students were engaged. A number of parents who attended the productions made it a point to talk about what the dramatic presentations meant to them. Especially important to many was the presence of minority actors, which noticeably expanded the audience for history.

Whether either of the plays is a good history lesson is harder to assess. The teachers were given packets with information about the plays and about the historical characters, and some suggested activities to use in the classroom before the students came to see the presentations. I would assume that the students who were well prepared probably "got more" from the dramatic productions, but we do not know how much of the preshow material was actually used. We do have a huge stack of letters of appreciation from the children, but they were most likely required exercises assigned by the teachers, though some of the kids were genuinely touched by the situations they witnessed. Drama offers a way to show historical events and people and to make actions and dilemmas real and potent. Local history must use every opportunity to present the past in a way that reflects the complexity of life itself. Sometimes fiction provides an important means of presenting the truth about the past.

About historical fiction historians tend to have two basic responses. One group utterly disdains it. The other group embraces it as interesting, as an alternative way of expanding the audience for local history, as a means of telling historical truths that cannot necessarily be documented in the sources, and as genuinely entertaining.

There have been times when historical fiction was our most popular literary form. George Dekker notes that over time "nothing has sold as well as historical fiction." Dekker points to Sir Walter Scott and his Waverley books (circa 1814) as the origin of the historical romance, in which the novel develops a historical consciousness by "multiplying the variety of natural and social forces that impinged on its characters' behavior."[5]

Ernest E. Leisy, who studied and categorized historical fiction, claims there have been three periods when Americans have turned to this genre. The first was the era following 1813 when the nation was creating its own identity. *The Spy* appeared in 1821. James Fenimore Cooper followed the pattern established by Scott in his portrayal of a family divided by partisan interests during the American revolutionary war. This first phase ended with the publication of *Uncle Tom's Cabin*, whose great influence has been acknowledged by many, including Abraham Lincoln, who is said to have referred to its author, Harriet Beecher Stowe, as the "little woman who started the war."[6]

The second period of interest in historical fiction, according to Leisy, was at the turn of the twentieth century. This era also saw the appearance of local color and regional novels, both of which depended on the development of place as well as event. Leisy identifies the third phase of interest in the historical novel as the decades between the 1930s and 1950s. The star attraction during that era was certainly *Gone with the Wind*, which Dekker cites as the most famous and best-selling twentieth-century American historical romance; Wharton's *The Age of Innocence* and Faulkner's *Absalom, Absalom!* were, he claims, "the greatest."[7]

Leisy defends historical fiction as more than escapist literature because "it satisfied many tastes," and it "satisfied the need of the human mind for a story." He sees it as full of suspense and drama, allowing us to read about people more fully developed than those in traditional books of history. Leisy believes that historical fiction satisfies the reader with its "color, pageantry, and the love of excitement."

What is true is that historical fiction has attracted writers of varying abilities and the stories are usually vivid and full of authentic detail. That detail, of course, is what tends to make historical fiction seem so truthful to its readers. Consider the reviews of *Cold Mountain* that commented on Charles Frasier's precise and often arcane vocabulary.[8] Historical fiction has also taken a prominent place in our schools. In preference to using books of history, some elementary school teachers, I have found, use historical fiction as the basis of their lessons. I talked recently with a fourth grade teacher who said her entire lesson on abolition and the Underground Railroad came from fictional accounts. This could be seen as a good thing because these books are full of small and telling details and are usually well plotted; it could also be seen as a failure on the part of historians to produce the sort of books that are useful to classroom teachers.

Historical fiction can enlarge the audience for history. The best historical fiction is well written, full of interesting details and stories, and peopled with engaging personalities. These are characteristics that need not be limited to fiction, however, for books of history can also be well written, full of engaging details and interesting characters, and they can surely portray the drama of the past. These are things we local historians need to remember when we sit down to write.

Local historians do a great deal for our communities in terms of answering questions, making people aware of the special places in which we live, and keeping the past alive and relevant to everyday lives. We communicate history in many ways. In return, we also receive a great deal. One of the most satisfying activities that aids me in understanding my hometown, and in knowing how I can talk about it with others, is looking carefully at the place where I live.

In good weather, I perambulate my historical kingdom, if you will, and so should we all. I walk the streets looking at the domestic architecture, the plantings in back- and side yards, the evidence of renewal, the loss of community services such as small groceries and repair shops, and the uprisings or the "down-goings" of an area. I think it is important to know my place on foot, rather than through a car window passing by at 30 miles or more per hour, racing to get to other chores, and paying little attention to detail. When we drive we *use* the streets of our home places, but we do not get to know them intimately.

I perambulate, the very word slowing me down, in order to appreciate what is here and what was there. I look at the evidence of the past that can be seen and note where the street or neighborhood is headed. I perambulate to understand the relationships between places in my city, the distances between places of work and workers' houses, between shops and homes, the distance to school and church. I do this to understand what it was like when this was a walking city, when trips were taken in horse-drawn carriages, then streetcars, and then in slow-moving automobiles. It is only then that the many small neighborhoods begin to make sense, when the duplication of services every few blocks takes on meaning, when I can gauge neighborhood shifts as new areas became fashionable and older areas attracted those less affluent.

I perambulate, too, in order to relive the stories of place. Mostly I walk about in order to recall the people of the past. I remember, at the corner of Plain and Cleveland Streets, Zachariah Tyler and his son John, who lived in two small houses, side by side, their homes metaphors for their partnership in life. In peacetime they worked together as whitewashers, but in 1864, father and son enlisted in the 26th U.S. Colored Infantry and went off to war. In 1865 they returned home from Texas where they had been discharged, Zachariah to preach in various A.M.E. Zion churches and John to become the local ice cream man.

On North Tioga Street I recall the day two workers lost control of a set of trolley wheels that went sailing unimpeded along the tracks into town, the workers racing along behind. I wonder what people thought as they saw those wheels spiraling past them. On North Albany Street I think about the hermit who lived for years and years behind one of the humble houses there, rarely coming out but visited regularly by his cousins, who arrived in swell carriages, and watched by the neighborhood children, perched in the large silver maple in order to peer into his shack. On State Street I think about one of the city's "Grand Dames" who was known in her later years as the "shopping lady." She had vowed as a teenager—though the term was not used then—not to get stuck in our city, but alas, she did, and she ended her days buying items from the downtown stores, which she carefully carted home but never bothered to unwrap.

At the park in the center of the city I recall the various uses to which it has been put: a place to declaim Independence Day; the public square where emancipation was celebrated; the site where George Johnson—a colored man, he would have been called then—gave an elegant oration twenty years later, naming those in the town who had aided the cause of the fugitive slave and those who had not. In later years it was a place of concerts and art shows. In the 1830s it was from this park that the Reverend Samuel Parker left on his journey to take the religious pulse of the Pacific Northwest, as did numerous other missionaries after him, including Dr. Marcus and Narcissa Whitman.

My perambulations allow me to think about streets and what they were named, how they were improved by the municipality, first with gaslights, then electricity. I consider the various laws enacted to clear the streets of animals, and later of snow; how the shade trees were to be protected from the depredations of horses tethered to the lower branches, and finally laws that regulated the speed of wagons and automobiles.

My perambulations allow me to see, by the arrangement of houses on lots, where serious gardens once existed, edged by fruit trees. And by extension, I can recall the work of planting, and weeding, and hoeing and can think of the kitchen work that followed harvest. I can recall property fashions, too, for at one time fences were important; they no longer are, and now few are to be seen. Today, what were once gardens are more often home to plastic swimming pools for the children.

Walking about helps me understand the idea of neighborhood, for even in my small city there were defined areas, each with its own name, its own character. The Missouri Historical Society pamphlet series about neighborhoods in St. Louis documents areas, and occupations, and ethnicity, highlighting growth and decline, and regrowth, and looks at architectural styles. These pamphlets help residents today understand where they live, and they allow those of us with knowledge about place to share it in an inexpensive and accessible format with people who might be unlikely to attend historical society lectures or exhibits.

Our older histories sometimes contain important insights about the places where we live—for an understanding of environmental change is not new. In his 1898 history of Dryden, New York, George Goodrich offers some significant commentaries that have long gone unnoticed but which explain the consequences of certain uses of the land. Dryden in Goodrich's time was a prosperous village supporting fifty-three sawmills, all run by waterpower. He noted that deforestation was necessary so that agriculture could flourish and the mills could produce lumber. Later, he mentioned that past winters in Dryden had not been as bitter as they were in the 1890s when he was writing because in the early days the heavy forest protected inhabitants from snow and wind. In the early days, he insisted, snowdrifts were unknown, but with the trees gone, the wind cut across open fields and piled snow as high as a man could stand. Finally, Goodrich explained that malignant typhoid fever developed throughout the area because the lowlands had been deprived of their natural foliage and the town had not yet established artificial or effective means of drainage.

Knowledge of place, an understanding of where we live, can bring pleasure to those who live there. But it is also a crucial factor in our sense of responsibility to the land, for to understand the past of an area is to foster current care.

We have returned to a consideration of the land where we live, much as William Lambarde did in 1576, when he wrote his book *The Perambulation of Kent,* and as George Goodrich did in explaining the changes in Dryden. Our hikes across the terrain of our home place link us to the land and to current historical interest in public space, the development of civic responsibility, architectural change, the market economy, and so much more. We perambulate in order to understand, to sense how a place was used in other times, and to see the consequences of that use so that we can communicate the complexity of the palimpsest on which we live to those who depend on us for understanding.

Notes

1. This book was originally published in England in 1788. It has been reprinted a number of times, most recently by Oxford University Press, Oxford and New York, 1993.

2. For essays about how Hollywood has used history, see Marc A. Carnes, ed., *Past Imperfect: History According to the Movies* (New York: H. Holt, 1995). There are a number of other books that deal with this issue. Two books by Robert Brent Toplin are important: *History by Hollywood: The Use and Abuse of the American Past* (Urbana: University of Illinois Press, 1996) and *Oliver Stone's USA: Film, History, and Controversy* (Lawrence: University of Kansas Press, 2000).

3. See Milton C. Sernett, *North Star Country: Upstate New York and the Crusade for African American Freedom* (Syracuse: Syracuse University Press, 2002).

4. From *Escape to the North*, presented by the Center for the Arts in Ithaca, during winter 1999 as part of the Hangar Theater's Educational Outreach program run by Lisa Bushlow, director of the Center for the Arts in Ithaca. In 2001, this program presented *The Day the Women Met*.

5. George Dekker, *The American Historical Romance* (New York: Cambridge University Press, 1987).

6. Robert A. Lively, *Fiction Fights the Civil War* (Chapel Hill: University of North Carolina Press, 1957).

7. Ernest E. Leisy, *The American Historical Novel* (Norman: University of Oklahoma Press, 1950).

8. Charles Frasier, *Cold Mountain* (New York: Atlantic Monthly Press, 1997).

Coda to Chapter 5

The Great Document Exchange

It has long interested me that in order to read about the early days in the Oregon Territory we need to go to New York State, where Narcissa Whitman's letters were sent. To know about English and Irish emigrants to the United States, and the lives they led in our communities, we need to search archives in Great Britain. To know what soldiers felt, how they reacted to the terrain, and what they saw when they went off to the Mexican War, we look not at battlefield sites but in the records in their various hometowns. So, too, we learn about the California gold rush by looking in New England, Pennsylvania, and Virginia for letters in archives and those published in local newspapers from Argonauts describing their crossing of Kansas, the intermountain West, or the Southwest. We find out about conditions in Florida during World War II by reading letters written home by soldiers stationed there: soldiers who, living elsewhere in civilian life, found Florida "something to write home about."

None of this is surprising. A letter from one person to another in the same town is rarely descriptive of place; both, after all, live in the community and presumably know what the area looks like, what is going on. This is not to say that local letters are not important; but it is to suggest that people look more closely at the local terrain when they try to tell others what a place is like. Diary keepers are generally more descriptive of place when they go elsewhere and create travel journals. The point of this is that in all our archives and repositories, even in the letters still in attics and garages, there is a great deal of information about "other places." That is, the place from which the letter was written, where the diary was created, or where the writer was at the time of writing.

Elizabeth Fuller, the librarian at the Westchester County Historical Society, a county 200 miles distant from my home, sent me a letter that had originated in my county in 1823. She asked me to write a comment about it for her society's historical journal.

What a delight! Here was a letter I knew nothing about, describing Enfield, a part of my county for which there is relatively little—well, truthfully, hardly any—descriptive material, at a time when the area was first being settled. Here was information about people who first farmed the area, about their doings, their origins. This is material that is very important for my community's historical record, but it resides in another place altogether. I knew nothing about this letter, and I suspect that other historians in my county do not either.

Suddenly, I had this wondrous vision. I imagined that one calm, sunny day, from all over the country, letters, diary entries, journals, and newspaper accounts would all rise gently from the communities where they reside, to hover and then flutter in the sky above. In my vision, the sky became full, and there were white envelopes everywhere, wafting calmly above the treetops. Then, softly, all these floating documents would descend to earth, heading homeward. (That I live in a community with a great deal of snow, and that this thought occurred in the winter, might have something to do with this miraculous epiphany!)

From that vision of rising documents, I conjured up the idea of a Great Letter Exchange. On some designated day, archivists and local historians everywhere in the country would draw from their local collections a single letter that describes another place. It could be a letter from San Diego when that place was a distant community struggling to survive, a newspaper account written by a visitor to an agricultural fair in Nashville, a letter telling about an execution held behind the town jail viewed by a traveler passing through Tucson, a journal entry describing Altoona by a traveler on the railroad, or a description of the irritation felt by the missionaries in Hawaii concerning the mores of the businessmen living there.

With the aid of a copy machine, the document would be duplicated, placed in an envelope, and sent to the keeper of that other community's history. Everyone in a careful, yet random fashion would give something, contribute something, to another community's knowledge of its past.

And just as casually, a day or two, or several days, later, the envelopes would arrive all over the country. An offering from Scarsdale might descend on Phoenix; an envelope from Norfolk would arrive in Independence; something from Portland, Oregon, might go to Portland, Maine; from Andover, Massachusetts, to Austin; from Chicago to Key West. From those envelopes, archivists and local historians everywhere would pull documents describing their own place—events and times of long ago, and not so long ago, with which they become richer. And in making this curious journey home, the document adds to the descriptions and knowledge of our communities and illustrates the links between us.

Can you imagine the pleasure of opening such a letter? Suddenly in your hands is a new description of your home place, a fresh view of something known or something new, an additional piece of the historical picture of the past that we are all, always, trying to add to—absolute completion being beyond any possibility. We would see our own history grow fuller, while, in addition, we would have evidence of a crucial lesson for our friends and neighbors. This Great Document Exchange would demonstrate the importance of personal observation, of writing, and of saving source materials. It would reiterate the lesson so many of us try to teach: that each and every one of us is an actor in history, a participant in times that will too soon become The Past, and that we are all capable of adding to the historical record.

Recently I saw a bumper sticker on a car that commanded me to "Commit Random Acts of Kindness." What a lovely thought. Perhaps the cars of archivists, preservationists, and local historians should carry a similar sign: Commit Random Acts of Archival Exchange. And who better than the American Association for State and Local History to promote this wonderful event? And all for the modest cost of less than a dollar.

The Great Document Exchange could become an annual event, and we would celebrate Document Exchange Day— perhaps during Archives Week. What a grand way to create national publicity and interest in local history. Now, wouldn't that be something?

6

The Local Historian

I summon to my aid the muse of local History—the
traditions of our own home—the chronicles of our
own section—the deeds of our native heroes.

—William Gilmore Simms, *Katharine Walton: or, The
Rebel of Dorchester* (1851)[1]

A local historian must be and do many things. If I were to ad-
vertise for a person to fill the position, my requirements would
mention some obvious skills and some that are not so obvious.
A local historian must be a multifaceted individual—with a
good deal of stamina—a person who is self-motivated and
happy working alone, yet someone who works well coopera-
tively too, a person who cares to get the whole story and to get
it as accurately as possible.

Local historians first and foremost engage in research. They
may specialize in land transactions of early settlers, in the impact
of technology on their towns, or on industries and products, but
they are generally expected to know something about just about
everything. Even then, a specific question might send them back
to the archives to learn more.

Local history research leads in many directions. Just as often
as there is success, there is the hollow knowledge that a search
has run its course, that the materials are just not there to be
found. In success or frustration, in traditional source materials or

in items we are just learning to use and appreciate, many local historians regard research as the best part of the job.

Local historians also collect and preserve materials. In places where there are officially appointed historians (most specifically Indiana and New York), this is often the most important official function they perform.[2] Seeking out new material and preserving older documents are important. Local historians are often asked for advice concerning materials that individuals and institutions need to preserve or interpret. They often answer questions about environmental concerns, concerning historic structures, or even the natural history of streams and rivers in a community.

Local historians communicate their interests and concerns in a number of ways, apprising the public of upcoming anniversaries, alerting people to the possible destruction of structures of historical note, teaching about the value of documents, and answering questions. These come in great numbers, even more now than previously as so many arrive via the Internet. Most of those are genealogical concerns; many are from the media; some are from preservationists; others come from researchers seeking documents; and any number of questions are asked by schoolchildren.

Local historians, who are usually defined by geographical location, need to know that history bleeds across borders and that there is much to learn even outside a designated place: people, after all, lived their lives without regard to town or county lines, so materials about one place are likely to be found in the archive there and in repositories nearby. Local historians need to read not only about their community's history but also about history in general, about other communities, and about topics. This sort of reading not only informs them but also poses questions that might be asked, demonstrates the use of different types of materials, and introduces topics that might not otherwise be thought of.

Theodore Zeldin, the historian of France, has noted that historians need "imagination" and that it is "as important to historians as new documents."[3] Professor Zeldin is not suggesting that we make up history but, rather, that we approach the documents of local history with the imagination to understand viewpoints of the past, to picture the landscape, and to breathe life into the documents we have.

Fairness and open-mindedness are especially important for a local historian. We cannot suppress material because we do not like it. We cannot ignore material because it does not fit set ideas—ours or anyone else's. We cannot be blind to contradictions that emerge. Often the written documents fail to substantiate an oral tradition—and such a discrepancy cannot be overlooked. Instead, inconsistencies need to be explored—and the long-accepted, but untrue, version should be explained. There is, of course, a lesson to be taught about that which is believed to be true but turns out not to be: it is the local historian who can demonstrate to the community not only what the records reveal (the truth) but why the other version (the local myth) took hold and then held on.

A local historian should see particularity and specificity in the past, but these should be placed in the appropriate context. Thus, a local historian turns a microscope on a geographic area to see how events known to be happening elsewhere were played out on this smaller stage. Thus we look for the effects of the Civil War even in places where battles did not occur. The good local historian uses a telescope too, to balance the delight of knowing particular things about a locality with a broad knowledge of regional and national history, so that events of one's town are placed in perspective. Not every local event is unique—but some are. It takes a knowledgeable historian to distinguish between the two and to know when to see a general pattern and when to claim something truly unusual. This balance is a crucial aspect of what the local historian must do. It is a task that calls for a microscope to see particular events and a telescope to see general patterns. So my want ad for a local historian would look something like this:

WANTED: Local Historian, skilled at reading history, asking questions, using historical imagination; needs knowledge of how to collect and preserve historical materials and how to pursue historical research; strong communication skills.

Knowledge of community important; open-mindedness, fairness, and perseverance a necessity.

There are occupational hazards that local historians face. A major hazard is that they research and write the histories of the communities in which they live, meaning that local historians often lack perspective on their subjects. Most academic historians do not remain long in or write extensively or exclusively about one community. If they do write a community history at one time, their next work is apt to be on another subject. Rarely will an academic historian pursue the history of one community throughout an entire career, although the exception that might prove the rule could be Blake McKelvey, who lived in Rochester, New York, for many years and wrote extensively about that city, or Constance McLaughlin Greene, who wrote extensively about Washington, D.C. Academic historians have a broader range from which to draw documentary resources, and most often they do not live among the people about whom they write. This gives them a distance that can be useful, especially when there are uncomplimentary things to be said. Local historians' closeness to place has its dividends and its drawbacks. Among the benefits is the close proximity of their sources of information—often their information even comes to them; they know the terrain and understand the close meanings of words and expressions that people in the area use; they know the probable places to look for evidence; and often they know the people—or those who know others—to whom they need to speak. This gives them an ease of access often unmatched for academic historians.

This familiarity, however, is sometimes a disadvantage. People in a locality usually expect that their history will be written in a certain standard, usually promotional, style. Few local historians care to broach topics about which there is community silence, for were they to do so the consequences could be extreme. The loss of local trust might put a historian out of business because sources can suddenly dry up and support and documents can easily be withheld. Consider the plight of Anna Rosmus, the

German teenager who turned from a successful history of her hometown of Passau to research its secret Nazi past. The 1990 movie *The Nasty Girl* is based on her research and her subsequent treatment by her neighbors when they discovered what she was up to. The townspeople were not interested in having their recent past explored and exposed.[4]

Our communities expect local history to be boosterish. Often local historians not only accept this view but allow it to color the type and range of topics on which they work. Of course, this is not to say that local historians are only interested in gossip or dirty linen. As one local historian wrote to me, most people in a community know the local stories—long before the local historian goes to work. What they do not approve of, however, is reviving the story, putting it into print, and making it available to others. Where is the line between gossip and historical topic? What subjects can and should be pursued in a local history?

What does a local historian do with dirty linen? In general, the specifics of a story are probably not of great interest to us as long as it remains a personal situation; when it touches on a significant celebrity in the community who has already given up privacy by taking a public role, then it might be considered. When a story typifies a trend, then the trend can be investigated. The uncomfortable bits are part of history too. We need to find ways of dealing with them. The Ku Klux Klan activity of the 1920s in the North is a subject that makes people profoundly uncomfortable, as does discussion of the race riots of the 1960s; yet tragedies—natural and those of human making—need to be dealt with.

Consider, for example, this situation from my local area. In the 1860s, a woman poisoned her two teenaged daughters and probably several others as well. There was a trial, and she was found guilty. She was sent to an asylum for the insane where she later died. Do we use the woman's name, especially considering there is family still in the area? Do we use the name when there is a local store known by that name? When I was going to write about this episode in an article about this nineteenth-century woman and crime, I mentioned it to the present owner of the store, who is no relation. He was glad to know beforehand but had no qualms about the name appearing in the local press as the incident had happened over one hundred years ago.

What if, on the other hand, a scandal involved some betrayal of the public trust? What if the heir of the town's most respected family caused the family bank to fail? Here the personal scandal becomes part of a larger picture and one that touches on the loss of the financial institution for the community and the consequences for people whose investments and trust it had held. In this case, the failure of the bank places the family in the middle of the story. "I would not write the story of such a failure," said one local historian to me with a glinting eye, daring me to say that I would. But I think that I might. Here, my editor challenges me: Would I now, as an experienced local historian, write about this episode? Would I have done so when I was just starting out? Well, both probably. Today I would write the story because I am interested in what happens to people when their savings are gone, when they need to start over. What public resources were there at the time to aid them? How did they cope? Did they remain in the community, or did they leave? When I was younger I would still have been interested in these same questions, and I think I would have written the same story. A bank failure is an important event. It affects the community, and it affects individuals. From such an investigation we can learn a good deal.

Peggy Korsmo-Kennon, director of the Waseca County (Wisconsin) Historical Society at the time when I met her some years ago, sent me an interesting problem concerning an individual's right to privacy. In a community history published in 1980, there is mention of a 1952 murder. Writing some thirty years after the event, the author notes that "few criminal trials have aroused greater interest" in the town. Included in the history are three paragraphs about the murder and the punishment meted out. There is also an excerpt from the trial proceedings that had appeared in the newspaper.

A problem arose, however, because the man convicted of the murder—an instance of domestic violence in which a police officer was killed—had served his time in jail and was, at the time of the publication, free and living nearby. When he read about himself in the history he promptly sued the sponsor of the book and the historian on the grounds that he had paid for his crime and therefore should not be tarred further by it. It is a murky area of the law, but, according to one legal scholar, "it is difficult for someone to win this kind of privacy suit unless the person can also show that some of the published information is false." Still, the instance is a caution; what we write carries a local impact, sometimes far beyond what we can envision.

The answer to the problem of a subject's privacy must be found by each historian in how the material in question is to be used and for what purpose. And there are always new twists on this problem. Helen Hooven Santmyer, author of *Ohio Town: A Portrait of Xenia,* an admirable history, discusses notes that came to her along with an 1886 and 1887 survey conducted by the Board of Health in which each home in the community was examined and its condition noted. Santmyer decided, "As for its scatological aspect—that in itself is material for pages of comment. It is a disillusioning subject, however, and best let alone." Too bad. That sort of information could prove to be tremendously revealing.[5] The local historian might use the data as the basis of a discussion of the health problems identified in the community at that time, of common home situations deemed worthy of mention, of education levels, and of race, ethnicity, and class. How were the problems addressed? What public measures were taken? Were there follow-up studies? We should fall happily on such material as a great bonus to what we know about times past.

Another common condition of doing local history is that most local historians work alone. There are usually but one or two historians in a community, and there is not necessarily communication between them. Nor do local historians, in general, talk with, compare notes with, discuss problems with, or debate issues with historians in other communities. All aspects of our work suffer because of this: we do not get the aid of others who might know something about the topic on which we are laboring; we do not get to make comparisons with other places; we usually do not have the benefit of someone else reading our material before it goes to press. We fail to have a sense of knowing that other people are thinking about the same issues we are or are even interested in the questions we ask.

In many ways, this isolation is lessening, as there are more and more opportunities for regional historical organizations, academic conferences, and seminars that pull historians together to talk to each other. But this is not always the case. There are some obvious ways of correcting this situation. The American Association for State and Local History provides a newsletter and a quarterly magazine, *History News,* in addition to annual conventions, that can provide community and information. The National Council on Public History publishes the journal *The Public Historian,* which includes reviews of books on local history in addition to helpful reviews of historical exhibits and films.[6] In addition, state historical societies are sometimes effective in setting up seminars and workshops for local historians. In some cases, there are regional agencies that provide service and forums of discussion about local history. It would be smart to join whatever groups provide the sort of help that seems appropriate and to gather nearby local historians together in informal settings to discuss announced topics. (Do see the coda to this chapter.) A great source of historical companionship and help is available on the Internet. Begin with H-Local at http://www. h-net.msn/~local and see what your state has to offer.

There is also an edgy issue for local historians in terms of what the community thinks of its local history, of those who "do" it, and how they should be compensated. In many places I know or have heard of, precisely because they study the community; members of the community regard the local historian as a public resource. I believe the reasoning goes something like this: what that person does is my history, the history of my community; therefore that person should give me any help I need—which frequently means that the local historian is asked to speak and contribute without anyone seeing the need to provide payment for that labor.

We do not, however, make speeches without a great deal of preparation; we do not write articles without research and then whatever degree of struggle there might be to write, edit, refine, and make it the best we can. We are anxious to get the material to the public; we are accustomed to answering questions. Yet were the school district to ask a psychologist to give a talk, there would be no hesitation in providing payment. When it is the local historian who is asked to take over a class, however, school officials are often surprised that payment might be expected. I suspect that we are partially at fault for being so free with our time and knowledge. We need to set a higher value on what we do so that other people will value it as we do.

This is not, however, a simple issue; nor is it one for which I necessarily have useful answers. If you are a local historian, value yourself and your work. Investigate what other self-employed people charge for their time and what they donate to their communities. Talk with local historians in other communities (if only on the Internet) about what they do or wish they had done. Be clear with yourself ahead of time so that you can be forthright with those who ask for your help. Be prepared to say: "I normally charge $X/hour for that type of work. Would you like me to provide a quote?"; or "I normally cannot provide such services for free, but I'd be happy to make a donation in this case"; or any number of responses to fit situations you can reasonably expect to encounter. If we value our work and communicate that to our potential audiences, then we have a better hope of changing old patterns.

The problem of giving information to others, which most of us do willingly, is that there should be some limits: there should be times when bells ring and we realize how far we should go, what exactly our role should be. The school district is often the source of a common problem. Let me give an example: One Monday I had a phone call from a ninth grader named Gordon. "Could you help me?" he asked. He explained: "I am writing a paper for my English teacher on Ithaca's history. Could we meet to talk about it?"

My antenna went up. "What is the topic of your paper?" I asked.

"Settlement," he said. "I want to write about who came and why. I have been reading about the Sullivan campaign. . . ."

"Those are two different subjects," I interjected. "Related, for sure, in some cases, but two different topics. How long is your paper supposed to be?"

About four pages, he guessed, but he did not seem sure.

"Well, then, we need to get a focus. What do you really want to write about? There is Sullivan's campaign and there is the settlement era. Do you know when settlement began?"

"Well, no," he said.

"What have you read?" He named the standard nineteenth-century county history that runs over a thousand pages. He certainly had not read all of that: no one has!

"The 1894 book?"

"That one," he said.

"And what did you learn?"

"That Sullivan's campaign is interesting."

"Indeed it is. But it really isn't about settlement, at least not directly. When did the military campaign take place?" I asked in my most teacherly voice. There was silence. I answered for him. "In 1779. When did the revolutionary war end?" I asked again.

"1776?"

"1783. Settlement began out here in the early 1790s."

"Oh," he said.

"So pick one: Sullivan or settlement. You only have four pages, remember."

"Well, I am interested in the settlement era, why people came out here."

"Okay. That's good. Now what do you know about that?"

"Well," he began, and then there was silence.

"Okay. Let's focus on who came and why. Does that interest you?"

"Yes."

"Do you know anything about the Military Tract?"

"I have heard of it . . . I think."

"Okay. The Military Tract was land given to veterans of the revolutionary war as payment for their service. The state didn't have any money to pay the soldiers, so many of them fought with the promise of getting land afterwards."

"So they came out here?"

"Well, not so fast. Some did. Some didn't. In fact, probably most of those who got land didn't. So we have to figure out why."

"Why?"

"Well, you and I can figure that out after you read a little about the period and you write down what the topic is that you are interested in—just on a slip of paper, so you and I know exactly what you are going to do. By the way, how soon does this paper have to be handed in?"

"Pretty soon, I guess. Friday?"

"Okay. We'd better get to work."

Now I know that you are not interested in the local history of my place, but this scenario can be heard from Alaska to Florida, with the events changed but the players the same. And this episode involves some real problems that local historians and teachers have to face.

The first concerns the assignments that teachers give to students, for they are not always clearly stated. Teachers often let students go off thinking that in four pages they can write the history of an entire town. The second problem concerns students' understanding of the assignment. We all know that no matter how well focused, clearly explained, and logical an assignment might be, students often go away not understanding what it is they are supposed to do. Librarians face this problem all the time—even in prestigious university libraries.

The third problem is that doing local history research is not easy; the materials are not always there; all questions cannot be answered; some questions are more complex than they appear to be on the surface; and students, especially those in the fourth and seventh grades, when local history is most often assigned, are not prepared for the use of original documents, the lack of information, and the conflicting nature of the material.

There is the additional problem of sending young students to very outmoded books when there are better texts available—often right there in the school library—but sometimes the teachers do not know the subject well enough to know what the pertinent resources for local history are. Suggesting that students call the local expert is an easy way out. This raises the problem of sending students off to find the local expert, which in this case turned out to be me. I am happy to help, we are all happy to help, but without knowing anything about the assignment we are apt to lead students to more material than they really need to look at or to more complex renderings of the material when they were directed to the topic for some other pedagogical reason having little to do with the topic at hand.

This problem is even more complex because if even one student, not to mention six or seven, gets a local historian or local historical society person on the phone, this can be very time-consuming. There is an assumption (that I often resent) that I should spend any number of hours with students figuring out what the assignment is, what the topic of interest is, and all the other processes that go into leading someone into local history research.

Sure, our job is to help others learn local history, and it is the aspect of being a local historian that I like best. But the annual inundation of questions from students can be wearying, especially when we have other work on our desks. Students *should* come to us. But they should come well prepared so that we do not have to do the work that they and their teachers should have done to begin with.

One solution is for teachers to consult with local history experts *before* handing out assignments. They might request a list of topics and sources that can be researched with some ease by students in their grade. Another solution is for teachers to experience local history research *themselves* so that they understand the process. This happens far too infrequently, and in a way it is our own fault for handing out information without involving questioners themselves in the process of doing history. The bottom line is that teachers need to understand historical research, and local historians and historical societies need to be regarded as history consultants and not as tutors. This is perhaps the easy answer to a complex question. At the very least, everyone concerned would benefit from improved communication.

The ideal solution would be for school districts to hire local historians to give local history seminars for teachers interested in using local history in the classroom. Were the matter at hand the use of computers, or new math, or reading strategies, school districts would have experts to teach the teachers before they needed to broach the subject in the classroom. The same should be true of local history, for as simple as it seems from the outside, we all know that local history research, while fun and rewarding, can be a can of local worms!

My interest in all this is to get the student, of whatever age, to a manageable topic that is possible to do successfully. This is no less a goal than the teacher has!

Notes

1. *Katharine Walton: or, The Rebel of Dorchester* (New York: Redfield, 1853), 2.

2. See David G. Vanderstel, "County Historians," in *Encyclopedia of Local History*, ed. Carol Kammen and Norma Prendergast (Walnut Creek, Calif.: AltaMira Press, 2000), 115–19.

3. Theodore Zeldin, "Personal History and the History of the Emotions," *Journal of Social History* 15 (spring 1982): 341–42.

4. *The Nasty Girl* is part of a trilogy. The other movies are *The White Rose* (1982) and *My Mother's Courage* (1995), directed by Michael Verhoeven. *The Nasty Girl* won several awards, including the Silver Ear Award at the Berlin Film Festival.

5. Helen Hooven Santmyer, *Ohio Town: A Portrait of Xenia* (New York: Harper and Row, 1984), 90.

6. *The Public Historian* has been edited at the University of California at Santa Barbara since 1978. It contains articles and reviews of recent books, films, and museum exhibits; and often there are essay debates that present a variety of views. See, in particular, the roundtable devoted to the subject of public history and memory, particularly Michael Frisch, "What Public History Offers, and Why It Matters," *The Public Historian* (spring 1997): 31–40. The address of this journal is in care of the editor, Department of History, University of California, Santa Barbara, CA 93106-9410. See also Alan S. Newell, "Public History," in *Encyclopedia of Local History*, 383–86.

Coda to Chapter 6

Adult Local History Workshops

There are many routes people take to become local historians. Some are born into the position: "Dad was, and now I am." Others find the title thrust upon them: "When Mother died I found people just assumed that I would take over, especially since I inherited her records, so they call me when they have questions." These might be considered Wallace Stegner's rooted people—those for whom he had some envy because he considered his own background more of the bare-root variety. His family, like a nursery-bred rhododendron, moved about from town to town as his father sought work.

Others find that curiosity leads them to find out about a facet of the community, and that becomes enough to establish them as "experts" to whom others come for information. Knowing one thing often leads to becoming interested in knowing how to find out other things. Sometimes this path is taken by newcomers seeking information and involvement with a new place—an example of one of Stegner's bare-rooted people taking hold. Genealogical and architectural interests often lead people into local history research.

Some teachers find themselves unprepared but, nonetheless, are asked to teach local history. That experience, with too little information and lacking a prepared curriculum, often leads to a greater involvement with local history. Some people majored in history in college or liked it in high school and find that doing local history is a way of continuing that interest even if their professional lives take other turns. Others live near the historical society and are pulled in by programs or interesting exhibits. There are some, of course, who go to school expecting to work in the local history or public history field. These are people who learn a wide variety of useful skills and can move from one community to another in order to practice their craft.

Regardless of the roads that people take to become local historians, once established as local authorities, most assume a posture of immortality. That is, many people who have become local historians fail to take into consideration the fact that they will not last forever. So while local historians collect, protect, educate, exhibit, research, and write about the history of place, rarely do they take the time to wonder who will take over when it comes time for them to transfer to the great Archive in the Sky—or wherever it is that local historians go.

Rarely do local historians regard it as their duty to train others to take over the tasks of doing local history. It is easier to assume that other people will find their way into local history in the same haphazard way that they did. And it might happen.

But wouldn't it be far better if, instead of relying on chance, we actually thought of preparing for the future while we are still here to comment on that trove of letters in old Mrs. Smith's attic that one needs to keep an eye on, or to advise about the unreliability of the standard late-nineteenth-century history of the town, or to pass on that one crucial fact in order to follow the current thinking about The Big Local Topic? In other words, wouldn't it be nice to have a word or two with one's successor?

Wouldn't it be a gift to the person who follows to know that he or she does not need to learn everything all over again, as we had to do, but could come prepared, knowing how to conduct local research, how to ask good questions about a place, how to put the locality in a regional and even a national context? Wouldn't it be a good idea if local historians took on apprentices? Or, barring that, if local historians conducted classes or exercises to teach others the skills?

One solution, and it might not be everyone's, is to invite applicants to join an adult local history workshop. These should be limited to a small number of people; there need be no costs; and participation for the duration of a year should be expected.

Participants may come from those long rooted in the community or the recently replanted. In either case, it is interest and dedication that are most wanted.

A number of topics might be given to the group to consider, and, within a reasonable amount of time, the group would be asked to decide which one to take on. Some possible topics might include

- the depression of the 1930s

- our county in the Civil War era

- World War II and our locality

- the political history of our county

- race and ethnicity in our locality

These are broad but also clearly defined topics. I would expect the discussion of which topic to select to involve everyone in the group and to focus on how one goes about learning something about the locality. This exercise would be an important lesson in itself.

Once a topic has been decided upon, the group would engage in background reading, determine a work plan, and divide the research tasks among individuals or assign them to one or two people who might want to work together. This second phase might take several months as each aspect of the topic is explored. Monthly reports would reveal the aspects of the research that need to be refined and would help keep everyone up-to-date with all parts of the research. These meetings could also provide minor deadlines so that work progresses steadily.

While the research phase is under way, there should be discussions of what else needs to be explored, where to find additional information, what might be available elsewhere, and how best to communicate the results of the work. It might be that the topic and material should be shared in visual ways, or that something should be written up, or that the subject would work best as an ongoing dialogue that might occur in a number of places such as at a local historical society, in the newspaper, in the schools, or on the local television station. It might also be possible, depending on the skills of the participants, to have a variety of ways of disseminating the information gathered and the conclusions drawn about the topic.

Throughout, the goal for the participants would be to understand the topic. But the secondary goal, in my view, is to enhance the research expertise of the group and develop thinking about ways of dissemination. These are valuable tools that will easily carry over into other projects. At some point, it will be easy for the group's leader to step aside, knowing that there is a trained group of people who can comfortably take over the researching and communicating of local history.

This workshop idea is not new. In England there have been a series of Adult Local History Workshops held on a variety of topics aimed at exploring local history and at the same time teaching local history techniques. If you are interested, you might look at *Group Projects in Local History*, edited by Alan Rogers and published in 1977 by Dawson Publishing, Kent, England.

The English have devised some interesting ways of educating people interested in local history. In this country we have thought less about such things. A local history workshop might provide one relatively easy means of providing education in a context that is friendly, supportive, and interesting, in addition to being useful for the community. There are other ways as well. The municipal historians in my county have each invited someone to act as their deputy: this person is without municipal appointment but joins in all the meetings and activities undertaken by the appointed historians. They would be fine candidates for the positions when the current officeholders retire. We need to take every opportunity available to pass along not only the skills of local history but the joy of doing it as well.

7

The Past That Was Yesterday

Willing oneself into nostalgia for the present can, at
times, make one see the beauty of what is near at hand.
The world is still here for us.

—Howard Mansfield, *In the Memory House*[1]

There is little doubt that for the past twenty-five years, local history has been on a roll. It has been recognized, funded better than
ever before, of interest to a wide range of people, and it has been
proven useful. Local history has been written and it has even
been read; it has provided source materials for students, and in it
scholars have discerned patterns and models. I would date the
revival of interest in local history—or perhaps I should say a
broadly based concern for it—to the bicentennial of the American
Revolution in 1976: an easy date to focus on and one that creates
a tidy quarter century of time for our consideration.

This was not the situation for local history earlier. Prior to
1976, local historical societies were—in general—doing things as
they had always been done: membership was restricted by habit
to local elites, to those who found antiquarian pursuits compat-
ible, and to the elderly—or at least those over the age of fifty.
Few historical societies did more than collect the artifacts of
prominent families, sponsor lectures that were in general poorly
attended, and host genealogists who came to use the documents
kept in historical society archives. I do realize that there were
some exceptions, but, in general, historical societies were rather

musty places. They were dependent on a few who, over and over again, elected themselves to the boards of trustees; they reached out almost not at all; and they expected to continue with dim lighting and inadequate captions for objects that were rarely dusted or replaced. They were places visited by schoolchildren, places occupying old houses or rooms somewhere, places that survived on infusions of money from wills and trusts and membership dues of $2.00 or $5.00.

The local history written at that time, though shorter, tended to mimic the histories of the nineteenth century. The topics that came under consideration were much the same as those in earlier days. Public talks tended to focus on battles, on Indians, on archaeological ruins, or on local industries. The staff was usually volunteer, and those who were paid were mostly untrained.

What local history had in those days was stuff. Much of it was inadequately housed, not all of it was cataloged, but it was preserved and was considered a local treasure. Those were the days of lantern slides, of rows of exhibit cases containing rows of arrowheads and other items lined up one by one, and of talks read from long handwritten pages. I do know what I am talking about because I knew those places well. I began doing local history in that antediluvian era, and I loved it. But the winds of change were blowing, and I loved that too.

We all know the pitfalls of dating a trend to a precise time, and though I contend that things began to change in 1976 when the United States celebrated the bicentennial, the roots of and reasons for that change are embedded in earlier times. By 1976 a variety of trends, people, interests, and concerns came together to effect a change in local history, creating a vibrant field of inquiry.

Of great importance is that, by the 1960s, the academic profession of history was itself giving birth to new forms and interests. The origins of this can be found with the activities of the *Annales* School in France. Beginning in the late 1920s, a number of French historians looked beyond military, political, and diplomatic events to consider social and economic forces on people and on times. These historians—Marc Bloch and Lucien

Febvre, then Fernand Braudel in the next generation, and Emmanuel Leroy Ladurie in the next—stressed the need to see *histoire totale*—or a history explored by using a variety of sources and historical techniques. This history made its way into the world of American scholarship following World War II.

Also in the world of scholarship, there was the twentieth-century development of the field of urban history, reflecting that, as historian Richard Hofstadter has commented, "the United States was born in the country and has moved to the city." Historians noting this demographic shift began asking questions about population concentration, industrialization, function, and the development of culture and society in America's urban places. Urban history was informed by sociology and issues then current in U.S. city life. In 1933 Arthur M. Schlesinger Sr. published *The Rise of the City, 1878–1898,* and in the decades that followed the field grew exponentially.

In England, George Hoskins (1908–1992) and H. P. R. Finberg (1900–1974), who established the Department of English Local History at Leicester University, defined local history in that country. English demographic historians created the Cambridge Group in 1964 to study household and family composition by using census and tax lists, baptismal records, and other statistical information. Their methods caused a stir in American academic circles, as did the books of English historian E. P. Thompson (1924–1993).[2]

In addition, by the 1960s there was well in place among American historians something called the new social history, which drew from and expanded on all these historical influences. In the 1970s, graduate students moved from campus to community in search of hitherto ignored documents and new lines of inquiry. The new social history opened exciting areas of investigation, expanding the cast of characters whose histories might be examined and advocating new source materials and new methods.

This activity among academic historians had implications for local history as scholars appeared in local archives, looked at local sources, and used them differently than before. The questions asked by the academy were soon being considered on the local level. It is perhaps in the field of women's history that the change might be best documented. There were women in historical societies, and most local archives contained materials created by or about women, though much of this information had been considered of little value. The publication in 1971 of the first three volumes of *Notable American Women* sent local historians in search of the notable women of their own places. This energy soon spread to investigations of ethnicity and race as the cast of characters of interest to local historians expanded.

What the academic historians were doing was only one influence on the local scene, for the academic historians, as well as those in localities, were exploring topics that were also part of the national political agenda in that era of America's second war on itself—the era of civil rights and antiwar protest. The rise of black power, women's rights, and the American Indian movement can be seen reflected in the questions historians asked and gave rise, eventually, to the historical trends that dominated the last quarter of the twentieth century.

The preservation movement must also be credited with stimulating an interest in and a use for local history. Although preservation activities could be found in the nineteenth century, the National Trust for Historic Preservation became potent in the 1960s, especially after the passage of the National Historic Preservation Act of 1966, which energized preservation activity all over the country. The focus moved from Mount Vernon—and other similar special places—to Main Street. The preservationists had to become activists to persuade communities of the value of identifying and maintaining our architectural heritage, and in fighting those battles they needed to delve into the records to document threatened structures. This brought a great deal of new energy and a bevy of active people into the historical archive. Although local history and preservation might have become partners working from one base, in most cases the local historians were uncomfortable with the confrontational tactics of the preservationists and the preservationists were impatient with the stodgy, careful approach taken by those in historical societies. Generally, in most places two organizations evolved. What the preservationists achieved was a visibility for the architectural remains of the past, reclaimed and then put back into use. They focused on the use of local documents and local information, clearly articulated for the community. They were, in the long run, good for our communities and good for local history.

Along with preservation, the 1960s experienced *Foxfire*, an innovative teaching technique that sent children into their neighborhoods to uncover and preserve folkways still being practiced. *Foxfire* spread from Georgia, where it began in Raban Gap, to schools around the country. It coincided with an expansion of academic interest in folklore. By 1975 the concept of "Small Is Beautiful" focused on life outside of large urban centers just as some Americans began to investigate what was called an "alternative lifestyle."[3]

Other things also worked to promote the local. History Day began in 1974 and challenged students to create local history projects. The National Endowments, chartered in 1965, received greater funding and directives to become more responsive to localities. By the mid-1970s they had spawned state arts and humanities councils with funding distributed statewide by decentralized programs. This challenged and improved local history because, to get grants, the standards of the councils had to be met. For the first time, in many cases, organizations regularized boards of directors, terms of appointment, and training. To be competitive, history projects of all sorts had to be carefully thought through, and experts needed to be consulted and hired. For local history to be competitive, it had to be more professional. All of this was good for the independent scholar and historical agency alike. Also during that era, the Newberry Library of Chicago sponsored a series of Local and Family History Seminars that stressed historical techniques, including quantitative skills and a familiarity with computer use—then something of a surprise to historians, now indispensable.

In 1976 the public history program at the University of California at Santa Barbara ushered in a new era by preparing students for careers in state and county historical societies and in government and industrial archives. Beginning in 1979, *Cobblestone Magazine* brought lively and topical historical issues to children. Regional programs also appeared: the Appalachian Studies Center, the Long Island Studies Association, the Center for Great Plains Studies, and the Center for the Study of Southern Culture. All of these developments, and others, fostered a sense of the importance of the local.

On bookshelves there were new books of local history, and more were planned, while older, standard histories were reprinted or indexed. Historical societies, long dormant, saw that they had something important to offer their communities; community colleges began listing courses in local history; and in many states local history offerings in the public schools were relocated into the elementary grades, where those teaching them were challenged to improve the quality of their lessons, thereby producing a new emphasis on Native Americans, on ethnic groups in the community, and sometimes on women of note.

All of this was going on at the same time that this country celebrated the bicentennial of the American Revolution. By 1976, despite national commissions and programs, most people realized that the only meaningful celebrations would be those in America's localities. Local committees formed, celebrations were planned, and except for the appearance of the tall ships on national television, most of the memorable aspects of the bicentennial occurred at home.

Most significant during the past quarter century was the impact of the publication of *Roots* and its broadcast as a television series in 1976–1977. Alex Haley's story of Kunta Kinte, his abduction from his African home, his days of slavery, and his family thereafter riveted viewers and spawned an interest in genealogy among people of varying backgrounds. The abiding importance of *Roots* is not in Haley's dramatized genealogy, although that did stir emotions in a great number of people, but, rather, in the fact that an African American was able to put names and places on his ancestry. This propelled others into the field; people who might have thought that their ancestries were impossible to track, or too recent or insignificant to locate, became interested in their own backgrounds. Suddenly, the microfilm room in the National Archives, long the haunt of genealogists seeking family connections for admission to elite organizations, became the haunt of young and elderly, of black and white, of those whose families had come to this country during the twentieth century as well as those who had arrived on the *Mayflower*. The second stunning shift in genealogy, of course, occurred in the 1990s with widespread computer use and the links made possible by the Internet. Today it is estimated that there are more than seventeen million people all over the country involved in researching aspects of their family histories.

Over the past quarter century history has blossomed. Television featured Charles Kuralt's programs about localities and local personalities, the *American Experience* brought history stories to public television, and the History Channel appeared and proved to be very popular. For Americans, participation has always been more attractive than simply being part of an audience, and while children played with G.I. Joe and Barbie, many adults threw themselves into revolutionary and Civil War battle reenactments, complete with careful attention paid to uniforms and equipment and troop organizations replicating those of the original battlefield.[4] In 1990, Ken Burns gave us *The Civil War* on public television, followed by other programs that relied on the voices and visuals of participants, another reinforcement of the importance of the individual and of local documents.

Tourism flourished too. Our national parks were visited by greater numbers than ever before. Taking notice of changing historical fashions, the National Park Service embarked on a bold program of revising exhibits to reflect new historical trends and developing new sites. There was the Lowell, Massachusetts, mill that became the first industrial National Historic Site, authorized in 1978. There was the Maggie Walker House in Richmond, Virginia, celebrating the life of a woman from a humble background who pioneered in hair-care products for African Americans. Eventually, in the late 1990s, the concept came into being of a noncontiguous park to commemorate the many places and people important to the abolition movement and the Underground Railroad. In addition, the exhibits and labels at national park sites underwent a transformation, stressing inclusivity of gender, race, and ethnicity and the situational problems of events. There was, in addition, a blossoming of new and smaller museums and historical societies, sometimes fostered by the need to preserve a building, often spurred by the belief that state and county historical associations were not interested in the really local story. These were places where the professionalization of local history was eschewed in favor of local hands-on control and direction.

There were historical controversies, too, during the past quarter century—sometimes small affairs, sometimes large—that erupted into the public sphere. It suddenly seemed as if things historical mattered. There was loud discussion during the planning stages for the 1992 Columbian Celebration. In this case, questions were raised about the intent and meaning of the celebration, about whose history was being celebrated, and about the fact that the "discovery" of the New World involved not a lost or empty continent, as was often portrayed, but, rather, a place already occupied by native peoples with vibrant cultures. The old verbal jousting between Scandinavians and Italians over who had arrived first on North American shores faded completely in the face of the new controversy.

History mattered when the Civil War battlefield at Manassas, Virginia, was threatened by development. In 1921, the Sons of Confederate Veterans established a park on the site. In 1940, the federal government gained control of the land and created Manassas National Battlefield Park. From that time forward, the site was dogged by problems, culminating in 1993 when the Walt Disney Company announced plans to construct a theme park just northwest of the battlefield. Alerted by the media and the National Trust for Historic Preservation, historians came forward to defend the importance of safeguarding the park, and the controversy was played out in the press. Positions hardened: a Senate hearing was held, battle lines drawn, and, in 1994, Disney withdrew.[5]

There was also controversy about the renaming of the site of George Custer's 1876 battle. The history of that name is actually interesting and telling. In 1879 the secretary of war established the site as a national cemetery to protect the graves. Then, in 1886, it was designated the National Cemetery of Custer's Battlefield Reservation in order to include burials from other battles, and in 1926 it had appended to it the Reno-Benteen Battlefield. In 1940 the site was transferred from the War Department, and in 1946 it was redesignated as Custer Battlefield National Monument. In 1991 the National Park Service renamed the site the Little Bighorn Battlefield National Monument, reflecting the fact that there had been two sides involved in the battle—two very different points of view.[6]

History mattered again when historians at the Smithsonian Institution's National Air and Space Museum, on the Mall in Washington, D.C., set out to examine the use of the A-bomb against Japan in August 1945. There were, Tom Engelhardt and Edward Linenthal have noted, "two stories—of a weapon that brought peace and victory, and of a weapon that brought destruction and fear to the world." Objects to be displayed included the fuselage of the *Enola Gay*, the B-29 from which the bomb was dropped on Hiroshima on 6 August. The controversy was taken up by more sides than there are on a polygon: there were the historians who did not want to sugarcoat the past and for whom new material provided new insight; there were historians who believed that the scripts for the exhibit needed to be tempered; there were the veterans who had been in the armed forces in 1945 who were saved from possible death because the war was finally brought to an end; there were the American Legion and those with a military point of view; there were the advocates of World War II as the "good war" and those who were against all wars; there was Congress, from which significant funding for the Smithsonian flowed—or did not; and there was also the museum administration, baffled by the storm that broke all around it. In the end, and even after two exhibit scripts were written, the exhibit that was finally mounted in 1995, featuring and enshrining the *Enola Gay*, was "drastically scaled back." The controversy, which was played out in the media with many participants, was about the difference among "facts" and memory and careful historical consideration.[7]

History also mattered when the U.S. Holocaust Memorial Museum was chartered by Congress in 1980. The museum is dedicated to a subject that many people thought could never be displayed. Yet the museum curators innovated in concept and design, personalizing the horror of that era by giving faces to the victims. The museum staff also innovated with a startling Web site. The debunkers claimed that the Holocaust never happened; they placed disturbing advertisements in a number of newspapers, especially those on college campuses, raising the added issue of the ethical use of the press. Those whose lives and families had been directly touched by the horror of the Nazi past were affronted by the charges and testified of their pain and loss. Over these issues, there was loud debate joined by many voices, and history mattered.

There was, too, what has come to be called "the History Wars," waged over a number of issues but calling into question how history was being taught in the public schools, what should be taught, what sort of accountability public school teachers had to the taxpaying public, and the nature of history projects funded by the National Endowments. Central to the battle were the National History Standards, which had been developed by the National Center for History in the Schools at the University of California at Los Angeles with money from the National Endowment for the Humanities (NEH). The battle erupted in 1994 when Lynne Cheney, who headed NEH at the time the grant was awarded, turned against the standards even before they were made public. The problem, as Cheney saw it, was that the standards were "anti-Western, anti–Dead White Male, anti–free enterprise," and politically correct. History had democratized; it had become inclusive, aware of nondominant cultures and events, and in doing so it brought down the wrath of those invested in traditional historical topics and method. History, in this instance, certainly mattered.[8]

With interest in history at a peak, investigators discovered that historical knowledge among Americans was weak. So even as Americans visited historical museums in greater and greater numbers, at a time when books of popular history sold and people joined historical societies and reenactment groups, even while the American Girl dolls from different historic periods sold well and were collected by those who could afford them, and while genealogical fever spread, our knowledge of history appeared to be dismal.

What became popular during this era was heritage. We protected our heritage, we studied our heritage, and we exploited it. Companies offered heritage homes, heritage tours, and heritage dishes. We overdosed on the word, which came to mean, in the end, very little. So little did *heritage* mean that it was used interchangeably with the word *history*. People who collected family photographs were said to be doing history, and others who were interested in reenactments were said to be involved with history. These activities, however, were more likely to have been undertaken out of a personal interest in family or in battle uniforms rather than in learning and understanding as a historian would. Being interested in history, which is, of course, a good thing, is not the same as knowing or understanding history. Americans when tested are woefully ignorant of our national past; calling an interest in one's heritage history does not make it so. Historian David Lowenthal writes, "Heritage is not history, even when it mimics history. It uses historical traces and tells historical tales, but these tales and traces are stitched into fables that are open neither to critical analysis nor to comparative scrutiny." Historical knowledge looks at the past in order to understand it, whereas the heritage industry was interested mainly in exploiting it.[9]

During this era, history or historical sites became destinations. As our communities changed, from places that produced goods and products to places that could no longer identify themselves as manufacturing or commercial centers, those in charge of tourism noticed that history sites could draw tourists. Communities all over the country began to market their local histories, along with their festivals, natural scenery, sporting events, and museums, hoping to lure the casual tourist, the senior citizen bus tour, the convention, or the family out in the car for the day or a week exploring the countryside. Thus dawned the age of cultural tourism, usually directed by tourism experts, by tourist bureaus in chambers of commerce, or from a city or state tourism department.

How could all this not have an effect upon local history? Debates about history, the use of history, and the need for historical sites and an appreciation of those in a community; an emphasis on the local, the homemade, and the hometown; as well as a search for rootedness in a bare-root world, led individuals and communities to the historical society archive, to talks about the local, to an interest in preserving the local, and to questions about how this or that came about. That there was money—some money, not a lot—gave direction to the programming of historical associations and brought many of those organizations into a new era. That there was a need for scholarship led new people into the local archive where new questions were asked. A new alliance was forged between the academy and America's localities, and a genuine interest was created.

After years of historical societies scrimping to get by, and doing so with a minimum of community enthusiasm, historical societies, historic houses, and museums of all sorts began to turn up the lights and redesign and improve the captions on exhibits. This transformation was overseen by trained young people coming out of history departments and public history and museum programs. These were young professionals who were accustomed by training to think about history in new and exciting ways. They brought with them current historical trends, including interests in race, class, and ethnicity; in women; in the institutions of a place such as asylums, the distribution of charity, and the disposal of garbage; in the development of local government and of markets; and in the relationship of the local to the regional and national.

Historical associations have basked in this new attention, but they have also learned the value of cooperation. Now history museums join with other cultural institutions to promote the various opportunities for tourism in a community. This step has been fostered by the tourism industry and by the money that is sometimes available from tourism grants. In a sense, local societies have joined the communities they document, and being out in the streets, at meetings and public gatherings, has given them and local history a greater presence. People have come to value what local history has to offer.

Local history also appears in a variety of guises. Sometimes it is found in newspapers in the form of history columns, in objects of local history exhibited in the courthouse or in banks, as photographs that appear on buses, in programs on local access television, or on regional public radio and television stations. Local history is "heard from" when environmental impact statements are created for the development of parcels of land, when a building is threatened, or when a celebration is to be held. Local history participates in community life with the result that community members now expect it to be there—and this is a change.

And What of Tomorrow?

The important question really is not what has been created over the past twenty-five years but, rather, how local history is to maintain this popularity. How will local history and interest in things local continue to be popular, useful, and well enough funded to do a good job? How do we prevent local history from fading back into the more shadowy position it held after the turn of the twentieth century? How will local history fare in the twenty-first century?

Local history, meaning all those individuals, organizations, buildings, resources, and uses that have been found for it, needs to continue to function as a community educator. In addition to producing good books and pamphlets and intelligent exhibits and lectures, this means seeing and responding to community needs, being part of the local landscape rather than sitting apart from it, and cooperating with other cultural institutions and with public officials. It means that local history needs to understand the modern, living community it serves, not just the one buried in the local cemetery.

This also means not just informing people about the facts of what happened in their hometowns but actually finding ways to develop an understanding of the way in which history grows and evolves. This is not the same as giving an answer to a history question; rather, it is all about showing how the history of a place came about: the local influences and those from outside—national and international. It means looking at trends over time. It means, most of all, not treating the past like a golden era to be emulated and admired but, instead, treating it as simply the past. Education, I think, shows how the locality created its own palimpsest, each unique piece related to others that come after, each reflecting some of the universal, some of the homegrown, some of what came before. We need to remember all the various segments of the community that are in our charge, including not only the standard suspects but also local and county legislators, representatives of the media, and even historical organization board members who should be subjected to historical knowledge along with an understanding of the current budget.

The key to this, I am sure, is inclusion. That means inclusion in collection interests, exhibits, and lecture topics. It means investigating the history of a wide variety of people and situations rather than only the healthy, wealthy, and wise. It means opening the doors of historical societies to poets and musicians, making alliances with preservationists and others interested in place, answering the questions of local legislators even before they have the questions formed, and inviting groups into the historical society that have not been there before. It means looking at the outlying areas and helping them have a presence. The current trend of proliferation of smaller and smaller historical groups weakens central organizations and also dilutes the energy and financial underpinnings needed to keep one good society growing. It means, however, that when smaller associations spring up, as they have all over the country, hands need to be extended to aid them in their efforts.

Robert Archibald, in his interesting memoir of his life in local history, talks about this need for inclusion and his experiences with broadening the base for the Missouri Historical Society. Reading his book *A Place to Remember: Using History to Build Community*, especially chapters 6 and 7, should be required for all historical society directors and their boards.[10]

I have been struck by the enthusiasm with which people undertake genealogical research, generally adhering to high standards of accountability and thoroughness in their searches. I might quibble about the limited questions asked, but I am always impressed at the energy put to the task and at the amount of money they devote to their quests. There is energy, too, among those who become active preservationists. People don painter's pants and wield scrapers. Watching them become involved, become so intimately concerned, has made me realize that this same sort of energy could be and should be harnessed for the benefit of local history. We need to find ways of involving people beyond paying dues, visiting an exhibit, or buying a book. We need to extend to the local history audience the same privilege of getting involved in a more active way that is natural in these other pursuits. We tend to keep all the "fun" of doing history to ourselves and then deliver the results to the public. Sharing the research and planning and communicating about local history with others would be consistent with our role as public educators.

There are strategies that might be employed. Appointing a local history photography squad might be one for those adept with cameras. These folks could document the contemporary community, its festivals, its rituals, and its demolitions and natural disasters, as well as aspects of ordinary life. Photo squads could discuss what represents the community today, think of ways to bring community rituals to a broader audience, and create important documents for the present and the future. They should also be totally involved with the process of documenting—preservation, documentation, and display of their contributions.

Those involved with local history might sponsor or encourage groups devoted to writing a life history or writing about contemporary life in a town. It is our job to show others how their work fosters a knowledge of contemporary local history and to help them collect or copy their observations. We need to show people how the artifacts of the past talk to us today, how the documents of everyday life illuminate an era. These folks should have the satisfaction of contributing to the local archive, to local knowledge.

Several years ago we documented one day in my county. People were invited to write a diary account, tell the story of a neighbor's life or contribution to the community, describe the mall or main street, discuss teen slang, and tell local stories. We received more than six thousand entries in a variety of forms: diary entries, reports, essays, poetry, videos, drawings. When this same exercise was copied in the state of Utah, there were in excess of 500,000 entries. A number of other communities around the country have used variations on this theme, garnering priceless commentary about their places and also involving citizens in the process of creating history and knowing that it would be valued. This is a gift to the future.[11]

In 2001 our community created a shared diary. Noting that many people in December were buying diary books for the coming year, and knowing that within a month or two most of those books would lie in drawers as a reminder to people of what they had intended to do but had not actually accomplished, we devised a guilt-free way of contributing to a community diary. People were invited to offer up a diary account of any day or of several days or however many contributions they might choose to write over the course of the year. There were peaks and valleys, times when a number of essays would arrive and then stretches with almost nothing. In the end, however, we received a good many essays submitted by e-mail, by post, or hand-delivered. These detailed causes and ideas sometimes were reports made for local groups, and we even received the autobiographies of several people taking a class in writing at the senior citizens' center. These will be a treasure for historians in the future, not as much as we might like to have but more than we will ever have if we do not devise ways of showing people the importance of what each has to say and providing an archive in which their comments will be kept.

Adult local history workshops, as I discuss in the coda to chapter 6, are also valuable. They result in solid information about the given topic and a group of people who have undergone training. Some groups remain together to take on other topics; other groups function for one project and then disband.

The benefit of all these exercises is that what people contribute is shown to be useful and important, and in the process of working as photographers or local history researchers, people share their knowledge, learn about the sources available, and contribute to what is known about a place. Equally important is that those who participate learn about the nature of history—its shiftiness, its elusiveness, and its joys—and they grow in their understanding of place.

Local history has had remarkable visibility over the past quarter century. It has been nourished, expanded, and extended beyond a small group or a clublike setting; it is seen to be useful, and it helps define the community. It is up to us to see that this continues, not to keep ourselves in business but because the places where we live benefit when we and others engage in doing local history.

Notes

1. *In the Memory House* (Golden, Colo.: Fulcrum Publishing, 1993), 270.

2. See the entries for Hoskins, Finberg, and Thompson in Carol Kammen and Norma Prendergast, eds., *Encyclopedia of Local History* (Walnut Creek, Calif.: AltaMira Press, 2000), 186–87, 256–57, 434–37.

3. Elliot Wigginton created *Foxfire* when he taught in Raban Gap, Georgia, where he instructed his students to study the activities of people who were engaged in old crafts. The idea spread from there and was adapted by schoolteachers everywhere. The first *Foxfire* book appeared in 1961 from Raban Gap; after that there were at least eight books in the series, most of the later ones issued by various New York publishers. See John L. Puckett, *Foxfire Reconsidered: A Twenty-Year Experiment in Progressive Education* (Urbana: University of Illinois Press, 1989). See also E. F. Schumacher, *Small Is Beautiful: Economics as If People Mattered* (New York: Harper and Row, 1975).

4. See Tony Horwitz, *Confederates in the Attic: Dispatches from the Unfinished Civil War* (New York: Vintage, 1999).

5. See Joan M. Zenzen, *Battling for Manassas: The Fifty-Year Preservation Struggle at Manassas National Battlefield Park* (University Park: Pennsylvania State University Press, 1998).

6. The information about this site is from the Office of Public Affairs, *The National Parks: Index 2001–2003* (Washington, D.C.: U.S. Department of the Interior, n.d.). See also www.nps.gov.

7. See Edward T. Linenthal and Tom Engelhardt, eds., *History Wars: The* Enola Gay *and Other Battles for the American Past* (New York: Henry Holt and Co., 1996), 2. See also Martin Harwit, *Exhibit Denied: Lobbying the History of Enola Gay* (New York: Copernicus Press, 1996).

8. See Gary B. Nash, Charlotte Crabtree, and Ross E. Dunn, *History on Trial: Culture Wars and the Teaching of the Past* (New York: Alfred A. Knopf, 1997). The quote is from a review of the book by Michael Bérubé, "Our Children Deserve to Know," *The Nation*, 22 December 1997: 25–30.

9. David Lowenthal, *The Past Is a Foreign Country* (New York: Cambridge University Press, 1985); Michael Kammen, "History Is Our Heritage: The Past in Contemporary American Culture," in *Historical Literacy: The Case for History in American Education*, ed. Paul Gagnon and the Bradley Commission on History in Schools (New York: Macmillan Publishing Co., 1989).

10. Robert Archibald, *A Place to Remember: Using History to Build Community* (Walnut Creek, Calif.: AltaMira Press, 1999).

11. See Carol Kammen, ed., *One Day in Ithaca: May 17, 1988* (Ithaca: Ithaca Centennial Commission, 1989); and Shannon R. Hoskins, ed., *Faces of Utah: A Portrait* (Salt Lake City: Gibbs-Smith Publisher, 1996).

Coda to Chapter 7

One Last Thing

I would like to return to Marc Bloch's observation that to be a good historian one must know the present as well as investigate the past. Without knowledge and interest in what is going on in our communities today, without some understanding of human nature, Bloch warns that we will be only antiquarians. This is a wise caution and one I take to heart. I would add that because local historians are keen observers of the past of place, they might also use their historical skills to record and write about the present. Who better to turn an eye on a community to see what there is today? What better legacy to leave the future than a series of observations of our own time?

Before panic or rebellion sets in, I should explain that I do not mean abandoning historical research. Nor do I intend this to be regarded as a finished product. Rather, I like to think of our observations as a way of putting down thoughts about the places in which we live that will carry over to another time some of the flavor and texture of our era. There is a variety of formats that could be considered: observations might be a series of paragraphs in a notebook or on a computer, short essays kept in a drawer, photographs with extensive annotations, scrapbooks, or poems. What I am not suggesting is a diary or even a journal chronicling one's personal journey through life: that is another thing altogether. Rather, I am thinking of William Lambarde's *Perambulations of Kent* in which he noted what he saw—although his book chronicled one journey and what I have in mind is more of an ongoing commentary: short pieces about what is observed, paragraphs about the places in which we live.

These short essays would be general and specific at the same time. They would be personal observations, meaning they would reflect one view, sometimes bolstered with information from experts, such as the police for the number of arrests per month, the SPCA for the number of animals there at the time, the school board for the number of pupils enrolled in the local school, or the number of bus routes that serve the district. The election clerk could provide figures about the local turnout for municipal elections, with information from the newspaper. The goal would be for the local historian to identify things about a community that are important to that place, significant markers of change that has already taken place or is occurring, or what it is like to live in a particular place. These could be topics that a historical society director might assign a board of trustees to bring to each meeting or topics taken on by senior citizen writing groups or by youngsters in school; others can certainly be involved, but my interest is to have local historians think in terms of contemporary documentation.

For some people, this addition to the local historian's duties might cause discomfort, in which case the suggestion can be easily ignored. I will not show up at your doorstep and demand your notebook, nor will I send Federal Express to collect commentary from you. For other people, this sort of informal observation might feel unnatural because it depends not upon sources from the archive but on evidence of a different sort.

This type of writing is more personal; it depends entirely on the interests and abilities of each individual; it is empirical. And for the most part these comments will have a different texture from the documents in our archives because they are a planned exercise and not the sort of notations found in a diary, for example, wherein the writer has written what was probably believed to be a private observation, not one that started out to be more objective and public; or in letters, when one knows the recipient; or in other sources of a familiar type.

When I wondered about topics, I came up with a list three pages long and certainly had not exhausted the possibilities. What the list contains, however, are topics that extend how local historians think, observe, use their skills, and record. These topics begin with that which is contemporary but are actually informed by what we all know about the local past, and that gives these sorts of paragraphs special value, for they will be written with knowledge of place, an understanding of what was as well as what is. What informs this list—and it is far from exhaustive—is an awareness that local history is broad, that the topics to explore are endless, and that often we fall into thinking in rather set ways from which these suggestions might jolt us. As individuals we will all record what is of interest; we will act as current historians of place. We should enter into this rather conspiratorially, that is, we are writing specifically to those who will come after us. We are leaving ways of understanding the world in which we live to people in the future who will live where we do. This list might cause you to see your home place in a new light, and it could even cause you to wonder about the same things in the past.

Consider writing about

- community festivals that mark the year

- local signs of the change of seasons

- dangerous local places: natural and created

- things that change the skyline

- where you can glimpse the past: the uncluttered view

- the many communities to which you belong: geographic, ethnic, occupational, affectional or voluntary, extended family, linguistic

- sound history; what you hear throughout the day and also what sounds you remember from the past

- the local palate of odors: smells that evoke things today and those that make you think of the past

- remnants of our agricultural past: in some places this might be turned around to think about the small commercial centers that once were but no longer are

- routines of place: rush hours, quiet times
- meeting places: these will differ by age, occupation, and other factors (I am thinking here of teens in a mall, ladies at lunch, people meeting at civic groups, in churches, and so on)
- use of the land
- neutral places in a community: the library, perhaps
- shifts in shopping patterns
- traffic patterns: where the local bottlenecks are, what places to avoid at particular hours
- crime
- volunteer roles
- the elderly: what they are doing today
- infant care: who is doing it
- those out of sight: who is not seen
- who is now visible (I am thinking of the physically handicapped and how we have made places more accessible)
- entertainment
- anticipated local sales: it used to be the August white sale that people anticipated (in my community there is the annual book sale, which happens two times a year—the little sale and The Big One; special flower and plant sales; art markets; the farmers' market)
- casual selling: tag and garage sales, a form of personal object recycling
- what sits at the curb for the garbage collector
- local characters, doubtful ones and celebrities; people in groups
- parades

- what is valued: read real estate ads for a period of time and figure out what attributes sell local houses
- leisure: health clubs and the Y
- local culinary specialties
- anticipated weather disasters: spring floods, hurricane season
- places to which you take visitors
- large employers in the area and small plants, shops, laboratories
- specialty shops
- how people dress today: in church, in the courtroom, going to school
- patriotism: evidence of
- how money is raised locally for charity, the arts, the hospital
- what is offered on the road into town (we call it Elmira Road; most every town has a commercial strip leading into the town)
- things you need to buy elsewhere: shoes, music, jewelry, veal
- descriptions of the countryside
- seasonal events
- people who work outside: roofers, painters, car repairers
- who is picking up trash along our roads: enumerate the signs
- how a community advertises itself
- local groups
- alternative communities
- signs along local roads

- new road names: document them now
- the people using the library
- lost occupations and services
- bumper sticker causes
- yard art or yard ornaments
- reminders of the past
- portents of the future

This list could go on. We local historians are poised to recover the past for our communities, and we should consider documenting the places in which we live now, leaving to the future ways of seeing this time in both the particular and the general, descriptive and factual, photographic and written, in words that will illuminate our own times and give another dimension to the job description of those who enjoy doing local history.

Index

Abt, Henry, 92
Adams, Charles Kendall, 21
Adams, Herbert Baxter, 21
Adams, James Truslow, 28
adult local history workshops,
    156–59, 176
The Amateur Historian, 2, 9n1
amateur, 1, 2–3, 6–7
amateurs and academic
    historians, 21–22, 30, 34, 172
American Association for State
    and Local History (AASLH),
    34
The American Experience, 167
American Historical Association
    (AHA), 21–22, 150
American Revolution. *See*
    bicentennial and centennial
Annales School (France), 48, 162
anti-index, 102–5
Archibald, Robert, 174
Archives Week, 141

Beck, Henry Charlton, 106
Becker, Carl, 45, 47–48, 50
bicentennial of the American
    Revolution, 36, 166

Bloch, Marc, 35, 45, 47–48, 56–57,
    69, 162, 179
boosterism and local history, 66,
    146–47
Bradley, David, 74
Braudel, Fernand, 163
Burchkardt, Jacob, 3
Burns, Ken, 167

Callcott, George, 15
Caughey, John, 7–8
censorship and local history,
    59–63, 147–49
census, as source, 97–98
centennial of the American
    Revolution, 15, 17
Cheney, Lynne, 170
children, in history, 83, 93m
city directories, 95
Cobblestone Magazine, 165
Columbian Celebration (1992),
    168
community history, 15
Conference of State and Local
    Historical Societies (1904), 22
Cooper, James Fenimore, 132
Cowley, Malcolm, 27–28

crime, history of, 84
culinary history, 77–81
cultural tourism, 171–72
Curti, Merle, 33–34
Custer Battlefield National
   Monument, 169

debt, 83–84
Degler, Carl, 112
Dekker, George, 132
democratization of history, 16, 25
Dilon, Constantine J., 119
documents, problems with,
   50–53, 55
Dorson, Richard, 26
Douglass, Frederick, 76
drama and local history, 127–131

Eggleston, Edward, 21–22
Encyclopedia of Local History, 101
English Local History, Chair of,
   35
Enola Gay, 54, 59, 169
environmental history, 136–37
excise laws, 81–82

Faulkner, William, 132
Febvre, Lucien, 162–63
Finberg, H. P. R., 8, 11, 163
Flint, Timothy, 15
Food and Foodways, 79
Food History News, 79
footnote, golden rule, 113
footnotes: 105–13; sneaky 112
Fourth of July, 14
Foxfire, 36, 165
Frasier, Charles, 133
Frémont, John C., 115–16
Friel, Brian, 47, 53–54
Frothingham, Washington, 26
Fuller, Elizabeth, 139

genealogy, 166–67, 174
German nineteenth-century
   education, 21
Goodrich, George, 136
Goodwin, H. C., 13
Grant, Ulysses S., 15, 17
Great Document Exchange, 138–41
Green, Constance McLaughlin,
   33, 34, 146

Hale, Salma, 91
Haley, Alex, 166
Hazeltine, Gilbert W., 19–20
Headley, Russel, 27
heritage, 171
Higham, John, 17
historians, academic, 3, 6–7, 29,
   146, 163–64; influences on, 50
historic markers, 43–44, 117–18
historical associations, 20, 172;
   controversies, 168; trends, 6, 33
historical fiction, 132–33
history: change and continuity, 13,
   48–50; classical allusions, 16–17;
   of local history, 11–36, 161–77
History Channel, 167
History Day, 165
History News, 150
history wars, 170
Holocaust Memorial Museum,
   U.S., 169–70
Hoskins, W. G., 32, 163
Hough, Franklin B., 13
Howe, Henry, 15

Internet, 6
Irving, Washington, 16–17

Jameson, J. Franklin, 28
Jefferson, Thomas, 16
Johnson, Ben, 73

Johnson, Christfield, 23
Johnson, George, 135
journalists and local historians,
    31–32, 86–90

Kevlas, Daniel, 116–17
Korsmo-Kennon, Peggy, 148–49
Kuralt, Charles, 167
Kyvig, David E., 101

Ladurie, Emmanuel Leroy, 163
Lambarde, William, 11, 136, 179
Leicester University, 4, 35
Leisy, Ernest E., 132–33
Leuilliot, Paul, 69–71
Levinson, Sanford, 42–43
Little Bighorn Battlefield
    National Monument, 168–69
Local and Family History
    Seminars, 165
The Local Historian, 2, 3
local historians: appointed
    (Indiana and New York), 144;
    compensation of, 150–51;
    occupational hazards, 146;
    practitioners, 66, 143–55;
    prescriptions for, 2; women,
    26–27, 39n32, 39n33
local history: definitions of, 1, 3,
    4–5; diversification of subjects,
    167–68; future of, 173–77; in
    England, 4, 35, 163; in France,
    135, 62–63; modes of
    presentation, 121–37; in
    newspapers, 122, 124–26;
    popularity of, x; problems of
    doing, 7; reasons for, 14–16;
    research, 91–113, 143–44;
    subjects of, 17–18, 32, 34–35,
    65–84, 86–89, 179–84; trends,
    42–45

Lowenthal, David, 171
Ludewig, Hermann, x, 12

Manassas National Battlefield
    Park, 168
Mansfield, Howard, 161
Marty, Myron A., 101
McKelvey, Blake, 33, 146
Memorial to the Confederate
    Dead (New Orleans), 42
Monette, John Wesley, 15
Monfredo, Miriam Grace, 74
Monument Avenue (Richmond,
    Va.), 42
Mulford, Uri, 28
museum exhibits, controversies
    over, 54–55, 59–60, 61

The Nasty Girl, 147
National Air and Space Museum,
    169
National Endowments, 165, 170
National Historic Preservation
    Act, 164
National Park Service, 119, 167, 169
National Trust for Historic
    Preservation, 164, 168
Nearby History, 101
Nestler, Harold, 24
new social history, 35, 36, 163
Newberry Library (Chicago), 165
newspapers and local history, 12,
    14, 31, 94–95. *See also*
    journalists and local historians
Notable American Women, 164

Oliver, Sandra, 79–80
oral history, 37n8

pamphlets, 126–27
Parker, John, 71, 72–73, 76

Parker, Samuel, 135
The Perambulation of Kent (1656), 11
perambulation, 134–37, 179–80
Pitcaithley, Dwight, 119
place names, 44
political history, 82
Prendergast, Norma, 101–2
preservation movement, 164–65, 174
The Public Historian, 10n3, 150, 155n6
public history, 165
publishers, commercial, 23–26, 28

regional history centers, 166
research, problems of, 57–58
Robertson, Constance, 74
Rogers, Alan, 159
Roosevelt, Franklin D., 22
Roosevelt, Theodore, 22
Roots, 36, 166
Rosmus, Anna, 146–47
Russo, David, 26–27

Saltwater Foodways, 80
Sanborn Fire Insurance Maps, 98, 114n6
Santmyer, Helen Hooven, 149
Savage, Kirk, 42
Schindler's List, 74
Schlesinger, Arthur M., Sr., 163
Scott, Sir Walter, 132
Shaw Memorial, Boston, 43
Shils, Edward, 3
Shryock, Richard, 34

Simms, William Gilmore, 143
small is beautiful, 165
Smith, H. P., 24
Sprague, Stuart Seely, 71
state historical societies, role of, 6, 8
Stern, Jane and Michael, 81
Still, William, 72
Stone, Oliver, 127
Stowe, Harriet Beecher, 132
strikes , 83
Suffrage Statue, U.S. Capitol, 43

teachers and local history, 151–55
technology and local historians, 62–63, 63n2, 67–68
Thomas, Arad, 23
Tubman, Harriet, 76, 130–31

Underground Railroad: and local historians, 71–76, 130, 167; museum, 74; tour, 74
urban history, 33–34, 163

Van Tassel, David, 20

Walker, Dr. Mary, 44–45
Weilepp, Bruce, 81
Wharton, Edith, 132
White, Gilbert, 65, 121
Whitman, Marcus and Narcissa, 135

Zeldin, Theodore, 144–45
Zonabend, Françoise, 35–36, 70

About the Author

Carol Kammen has written and lectured about local history for many years. She has taught local history at Tompkins Cortland Community College and is now a senior lecturer at Cornell University, where she gives a course on Cornell history. In addition she has written three books about the history of her county, including *What They Wrote* (1978) and *The Peopling of Tompkins County: A Social History* (1985). The first edition of *On Doing Local History* (1986) was followed by *The Pursuit of Local History* (1996) and the *Encyclopedia of Local History* (2000), which she co-edited with Norma Prendergast. In addition, Kammen has written a dozen historical dramas that have been performed in Ithaca and regionally. Two, *Escape to the North* and *The Day the Women Met*, have been performed for 18,000 school children. For five years Kammen wrote articles for *New York History* about doing history in New York State, and since 1995 she has written editorials for *History News*, the quarterly of the American Association for State and Local History. She is a graduate of George Washington University in Washington, D.C., and she currently lives above Cayuga's waters with her husband, also a historian, and a feline companion, Carrie Chapman Catt.